DIFFERENTIAL
EQUATIONS

BY

H. B. PHILLIPS, Ph. D.

*Associate Professor of Mathematics in the Massachusetts
Institute of Technology*

NEW YORK

JOHN WILEY & SONS, Inc.

London: CHAPMAN & HALL, Limited

1922

TECHNICAL COMPOSITION CO.
CAMBRIDGE, MASS., U. S. A.

PREFACE

With the formal exercise in solving the types of ordinary differential equations that usually occur it is the object of this text to combine a thorough drill in the solution of problems in which the student sets up and integrates his own differential equation. For this purpose certain topics in mechanics and physics needed in groups of problems are briefly presented in the text.

The problems have been collected from a variety of sources among which the author wishes particularly to mention the Advanced Calculus of Professor E. B. Wilson and the notes on Mathematics for Chemists prepared by Professors W. K. Lewis and F. L. Hitchcock.

H. B. PHILLIPS

CAMBRIDGE, MASS.,
    Feb. 15, 1922.

CONTENTS

CHAPTER I

CHAPTER II

OTHER FIRST ORDER EQUATIONS

CHAPTER III

SPECIAL TYPES OF SECOND ORDER EQUATIONS

CHAPTER IV

Linear Equations with Constant Coefficients

DIFFERENTIAL EQUATIONS

CHAPTER I

FIRST ORDER EQUATIONS, VARIABLES SEPARABLE

1. Definitions. — In this chapter we consider problems involving two variables one of which is a function of the other. It is often possible from the statement of a problem to obtain an equation involving the differentials or the derivatives of the variables. Such an equation is called a differential equation. Thus

$$(x^2 + y^2)\, dx + 2\, xy\, dy = 0$$

and

$$x\frac{d^2y}{dx^2} - \frac{dy}{dx} = 2$$

are differential equations.

A *solution* of a differential equation is an equation connecting the variables such that if the derivatives are calculated from it and substituted in the differential equation, the latter will be satisfied. Thus

$$y = x^2 - 2\, x$$

is a solution of the second equation above; for when $x^2 - 2\, x$ is substituted for y the equation is satisfied.

An equation containing only first derivatives or differentials is called an equation of the first order. In general, the *order* of a differential equation is the order of the highest derivative occurring in it.

2. Separation of the Variables. — If a differential equation has the form

$$f_1(x)\, dx + f_2(y)\, dy = 0, \tag{2a}$$

one term containing only x and dx, the other only y and dy, the variables are said to be *separated*. The solution is obtained by integration in the form

$$\int f_1(x)\, dx + \int f_2(y)\, dy = c, \qquad (2\text{b})$$

where c is a constant of integration.

Since the integration formulas contain a single variable, if the variables are not separated, we cannot solve the equation in this way. Thus, if

$$x\, dy + (1 - y)\, dx = 0,$$

since $x\, dy$ cannot be integrated, we cannot obtain a solution by direct integration. By division we can however reduce this equation to the form

$$\frac{dy}{1 - y} + \frac{dx}{x} = 0 \qquad (2\text{c})$$

in which the variables are separated. The solution is then

$$\ln x - \ln(1 - y) = c.$$

When the variables can thus be separated the differential equation is called *separable*. An equation of the form

$$M\, dx + N\, dy = 0$$

is separable when each of the coefficients M, N is a function of only one variable or the product of factors each containing a single variable.

3. Different Forms of Solution. — The solution

$$\ln x - \ln(1 - y) = c \qquad (3\text{a})$$

can be written

$$\ln \frac{x}{1 - y} = c,$$

whence

$$\frac{x}{1 - y} = e^c = k.$$

Since c is an arbitrary constant, k is also arbitrary. The solution could then be written

$$x = c\,(1 - y) \tag{3b}$$

where c is an arbitrary constant. It could also be written

$$1 - y = cx \tag{3c}$$

or

$$y - 1 = cx. \tag{3d}$$

Any one of the equations (3a), (3b), (3c), (3d) is the solution of (2c), but of course the constant has a different meaning in each case and so two of these could not be used simultaneously.

Example. Solve the equation $(1 + x^2)\,dy - xy\,dx = 0$. Separating the variables, this becomes

$$\frac{dy}{y} - \frac{x\,dx}{1 + x^2} = 0,$$

whence

$$\ln y - \tfrac{1}{2} \ln (1 + x^2) = \text{const.}$$

Since any constant is the logarithm of another constant, this can be written

$$\ln y - \tfrac{1}{2} \ln (1 + x^2) = \ln c,$$

whence

$$y = c\sqrt{1 + x^2}.$$

This answer could equally well be written in any one of the forms

$$y^2 = c^2\,(1 + x^2),$$
$$y^2 = c\,(1 + x^2),$$
$$cy^2 = 1 + x^2.$$

EXERCISES

Solve the following equations:
1. $\tan x \sin^2 y\,dx + \cos^2 x \cot y\,dy = 0$.
2. $(xy^2 + x)\,dx + (y - x^2 y)\,dy = 0$.

3. $(xy^2 + x)\, dx + (x^2y - y)\, dy = 0.$

4. $\tan x \dfrac{dy}{dx} - y = a.$

5. $e^y \left(\dfrac{dy}{dx} + 1 \right) = 1.$

6. $x \dfrac{dy}{dx} + y = y^2.$

4. Derivative Relations. — In many cases one or more of the quantities occurring in a problem is a derivative. An equation satisfied by these quantities is then an equation containing a derivative, *i.e.*, a differential equation.

Thus it may be known that the slope of a curve is a given function of x and y. Since the slope is $\dfrac{dy}{dx}$, the curve can be obtained by solving the differential equation

$$\frac{dy}{dx} = f(x, y).$$

Again, it may be known that the velocity or a moving particle is a given function of the distance s and time t. The differential equation is then

$$\frac{ds}{dt} = f(s, t).$$

More generally, if the rate of change of a quantity x is known to be a function $f(x, t)$, then

$$\frac{dx}{dt} = f(x, t).$$

5. Determination of Constants. — Since the constant of integration may have any value whatever, there are an infinite number of solutions of a given differential equation. A pair of corresponding values of the variables is however usually known. By substituting these in the solution the constant can be determined and so a definite solution be obtained.

In many cases the derivative is known merely to be pro-

portional to a certain function $f(x, y)$. The differential
equation is then

$$\frac{dy}{dx} = k f (x, y),$$

where k is constant. If two pairs of corresponding values
x_1, y_1 and x_2, y_2 are known, by substituting in the solution
both k and c can be determined.

The statement of a problem thus consists of two parts.
One part contains conditions true at all places or times.
From this the differential equa-
tion is determined. The second
part contains conditions true at
a single place or time. These
are used to determine the constants.

Example 1. Find the curve
passing through (2, 3) such that
the part of the tangent between
the coördinate axes is bisected
at the point of tangency.

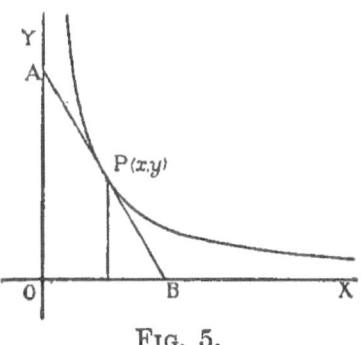

FIG. 5.

Every tangent is bisected at the point of tangency. Let
$P(x, y)$ be the middle point of the tangent AB. Then by
similar triangles

$$OA = 2y, \qquad OB = 2x.$$

The slope of the curve at $P(x, y)$ is

$$\frac{dy}{dx} = - \frac{OA}{OB} = - \frac{y}{x}.$$

This can be written

$$\frac{dx}{x} + \frac{dy}{y} = 0,$$

the solution of which is

$$xy = c.$$

Since the curve passes through $(2, 3)$, we must then have

$$2\,(3) = c.$$

Hence the equation of the curve is

$$xy = 6.$$

Example 2. Radium decomposes at a rate proportional to the amount present. If half the original quantity disappears in 1600 years, what percentage disappears in 100 years?

Let R be the amount of radium present at time t. The rate of decomposition is measured by $-\dfrac{dR}{dt}$. Since this is proportional to R,

$$\frac{dR}{dt} = kR,$$

where k is constant. Hence

$$\frac{dR}{R} = k\,dt$$

and

$$\ln R = kt + c.$$

Let R_0 be the amount at the start. Substituting $t = 0$, $R = R_0$, we have

$$\ln R_0 = c.$$

Substituting this value of c and transposing, we have

$$\ln \frac{R}{R_0} = kt.$$

When $t = 1600$, $R = \frac{1}{2} R_0$. Hence

$$\ln \tfrac{1}{2} = 1600\,k,$$

whence

$$k = -\frac{\ln 2}{1600}.$$

When $t = 100$ we therefore have

$$\ln \frac{R}{R_0} = -\frac{\ln 2}{1600} \cdot 100 = -.0433$$

which gives

$$\frac{R}{R_0} = .958.$$

This shows that 95.8% remains at the end of 100 years and so 4.2% disappears.

6. Differential Relations. — It is usually easier to find relations between the first differentials of the variables than between the variables themselves.   This is due to certain simplifying assumptions that may be made without affecting the results.   Thus, so far as first differentials are concerned, a small part of a curve near a point may be considered straight and a part of a surface plane; during a short time dt a particle may be considered as moving with constant velocity and any physical process as occurring at a constant rate.   The reason these assumptions give a correct result is because the ratio of differentials is by definition the limit of the ratio of increments, and as the increments approach zero these simple conditions become more and more approximately satisfied.

Methods of setting up differential relations in this approximate way are often called differential methods.   As here stated these methods apply only to first differentials, or first derivatives.   A correct equation containing second derivatives would not in general be obtained by considering a small part of a curve as straight and in a small interval a physical process as occurring at a constant rate.

Example 1.   Find the shape of a mirror such that all light coming from one fixed point is reflected to another fixed point.

Let the light from F (Fig. 6) be reflected to F'.   The mirror must have the form of a surface of revolution.   Otherwise light passing out from F in a plane through FF' would not be reflected in the same plane and so could not go to F'. Let PQ be an infinitesimal arc.   With F as center construct

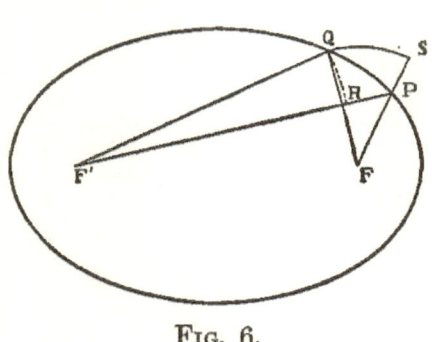

the arc QS and with F' as center the arc QR. Consider PQS and PQR as right triangles. They have the common hypotenuse PQ. Also, since the angles of incidence and reflection are equal,

FIG. 6.

$$\angle QPS = \angle QPR.$$

Hence the right triangles are equal and so

$$PS = PR. \tag{6a}$$

Let $r = FP$, $r' = F'P$.   In passing from P to Q the increase in r is

$$dr = PS$$

and that in r' is

$$dr' = - PR.$$

Hence, from (6a),

$$dr = - dr'$$

and so

$$r + r' = \text{const.} \tag{6b}$$

The section of the mirror by any plane through FF' is therefore an ellipse with F, F' as foci.

Example 2.   The sum of \$100 is put at interest at 5% per annum under the condition that the interest shall be compounded at each instant.   How many years will be required for the amount to reach \$200?

Let A be the amount at the end of t years.   In the short time dt the increase will equal the interest

$$dA = .05\, A\, dt.$$

Integrating between the limits $A = 100$ and $A = 200$, we get

$$\int_{100}^{200} \frac{dA}{A} = .05\, t \Big|_0^t,$$

whence

$$t = \frac{1}{.05} \ln \frac{200}{100} = 13.9 \text{ years.}$$

7. Flow of Water from an Orifice. — If there were no loss of energy, the velocity with which water would issue from an orifice at depth h below the surface would be that acquired by a body in falling the distance h, namely,

$$\sqrt{2\,gh}.$$

Because of friction and the converging form of the stream, the average velocity with which the water actually issues is

$$v = c\,\sqrt{2\,gh},$$

where, for ordinary small orifices with sharp edges,

$$c = 0.6$$

approximately.

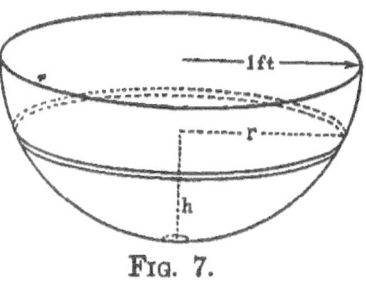

FIG. 7.

Example. Find the time required for a hemispherical bowl 2 ft. in diameter to empty through an inch hole at the bottom.

Let h be the depth of water at time t and

$$r = \sqrt{1 - (1 - h)^2}$$

the radius of the circle forming its surface. The water which issues in time dt generates a cylinder of altitude $v\,dt$ with an inch circle as base. Its volume is

$$\pi \left(\frac{1}{24}\right)^2 v\,dt.$$

This causes the loss from the surface of a slice of water with radius r, altitude $- dh$, and volume

$$- \pi r^2 \, dh = \pi \, (h^2 - 2\,h) \, dh.$$

Hence

$$\pi \, (h^2 - 2\,h) \, dh = \pi \left(\frac{1}{24}\right)^2 v \, dt = \pi \, \frac{0.6 \, \sqrt{2\,gh}}{(24)^2} \, dt$$

Separating the variables, we have

$$t = 120 \int_1^0 (h^{\frac{3}{2}} - 2\,h^{\frac{1}{2}}) \, dh = 112 \text{ sec.}$$

8. Equation of Continuity. — In a physical process there may occur an element which is neither created nor destroyed. The amount of this element in a given region only changes when some comes in or goes out through the boundary. In such a case the obvious equation

$$\text{increase} = \text{income} - \text{output}$$

is sometimes called an equation of continuity. Stated in differential form this may give a differential equation by which the variation of the particular element can be determined.

The concentration c of a particular substance is the amount of that substance in unit volume. If the concentration is uniform the amount in the volume v is then cv.

Example. In a tank are 100 gallons of brine containing 50 lbs. of dissolved salt. Water runs into the tank at the rate of 3 gals. per minute and the mixture runs out at the same rate, the concentration being kept uniform by stirring. How much salt is in the tank at the end of one hour?

Let x be the amount of salt in the tank at the end of t minutes. The concentration is then

$$c = \frac{x}{100} \text{ pounds per gallon.}$$

In the time dt, $3\,dt$ gals. of water come in and $3\,dt$ gals. of brine containing $3\,c\,dt$ lbs. of salt go out. Hence the change in the amount of salt in the tank is

$$dx = -3\,c\,dt = -\frac{3\,x}{100}\,dt.$$

The amount of salt at the end of one hour is then determined by

$$\int_{50}^{x}\frac{dx}{x} = -\frac{3}{100}\int_{0}^{60}dt,$$

whence

$$\ln\frac{x}{50} = -1.8$$

and

$$x = 8.27 \text{ lbs.}$$

9. Flow of Heat. — If the temperatures at the bounding surfaces of a body are kept constant, the body will ultimately approach a steady state in which the temperatures at different points may be different but the temperature at a given point no longer changes with the time. In many cases the temperature T is a function of a single coördinate x. By Newton's law, the rate at which heat flows across an area A perpendicular to x is then

$$-k\,A\,\frac{dT}{dx} = Q, \tag{9a}$$

where k is a constant called the conductivity of the material.

If we have a series of surfaces A such that the heat flowing across one flows across all the others, the equation of continuity has the form

$$Q = \text{const.} \tag{9b}$$

If then A is expressed in terms of x, the solution of (9a) gives T as a function of x. By substituting the values of x and T at two boundaries, the constant of integration and Q can then be determined.

Example. A hollow spherical shell of inner radius 6 cm. and outer radius 10 cm. is made of iron ($k = 0.14$). If the inner temperature is 200° C. and the outer 20° C., find the temperature at distance r from the center and the amount of heat per second that flows outward through the shell.

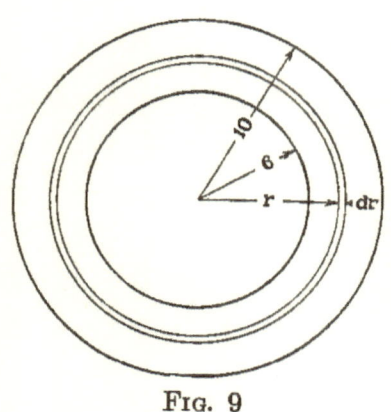

By symmetry the flow of heat is seen to be radial. At distance r from the center the area across which heat is flowing is the spherical surface

$$A = 4 \pi r^2.$$

FIG. 9

Since there is no accumulation of heat between the surfaces, the same amount flows across each spherical surface and so equation (9) is

$$- 4 \pi k \, r^2 \frac{dT}{dr} = Q = \text{const.}$$

Separating the variables and integrating, we get

$$4 \pi k \, T = \frac{Q}{r} + c.$$

Substituting $T = 20, r = 10$ and $T = 200, r = 6$, we find

$$C = - 1000 \, \pi k, \qquad Q = 10,800 \, \pi k,$$
$$T = \frac{2700}{r} - 250.$$

The rate of flow through the shell is

$$Q = 10,800 \, \pi k = 4750 \, \text{cal./sec.}$$

10. Second Order Processes. — In a problem containing two independent variables x and y it is sometimes stated that a quantity z is proportional to x and also proportional to y. What is meant is that, y being constant

z is proportional to x, and x being constant z is proportional to y. Both statements are expressed by the equation

$$z = k\,xy.$$

Thus, the rate at which a substance x dissolves is proportional to the amount of x present. It is also proportional to the difference between c, the concentration of x in the solvent, and s its concentration in a saturated solution. These statements are both expressed by

$$\frac{dx}{dt} = kx\,(s - c). \tag{10a}$$

The fact that the total amount of x present (solid and in solution) is constant gives an equation of continuity from which we can express c in terms of x and so express $\dfrac{dx}{dt}$ as a quadratic function of x. A process in which the rate of change of x is a quadratic function of x is called a *second order process*.

Example. Sulphur is to be removed from an inert material by extraction with benzol. By using a large amount of benzol it is found that half the sulphur can be extracted in 42 min. If the material contains 6 gms. of sulphur and 100 gms. of benzol are used, which if saturated would dissolve 11 gms. of sulphur, how much of the sulphur will be removed in 6 hrs.?

Let x be the amount of sulphur undissolved at time t. The concentration of sulphur in a saturated solution is

$$s = \frac{11}{100}\,\text{gms. sulphur per gm. benzol.}$$

The differential equation for x is then

$$\frac{dx}{dt} = kx\,(0.11 - c). \tag{10b}$$

If we use a very large amount of benzol, c will be very small and so this may be replaced by

$$\frac{dx}{dt} = kx \, (0.11).$$

Since x then varies from 6 to 3 in 42 min.,

$$\int_6^3 \frac{dx}{x} = 0.11 \, k \int_0^{42} dt,$$

whence

$$k = -0.15.$$

If now we use 100 gms. benzol, when there are x gms. sulphur undissolved, there will be $6 - x$ in solution and so

$$c = \frac{6 - x}{100}.$$

Hence (10b) can be written

$$\frac{dx}{dt} = -0.15 \, x \left(0.11 - \frac{6 - x}{100} \right) = -.0015 \, x \, (5 + x),$$

and

$$\int_6^x \frac{dx}{x \, (x + 5)} = -.0015 \int_0^{360} dt$$

$$\ln \frac{11 \, x}{6 \, (x + 5)} = -2.7,$$

which gives $x = .19$ gms. as the amount of sulphur undissolved at the end of 6 hrs.

PROBLEMS

1. Find the equation of the curve passing through the origin such that the part of every tangent between the x-axis and the point of tangency is bisected by the y-axis.

2. Find the curve passing through the point (2, 0) such that the part of the tangent between the y-axis and point of tangency is of length 2.

3. If in the culture of yeast the amount of active ferment doubles

in one hour, how much may be anticipated at the end of $2\frac{1}{2}$ hours at the same rate of growth.

4. If the activity of a radioactive deposit is proportional to its rate of diminution and is found to decrease to $\frac{1}{2}$ its initial value in 4 days, find the value of the activity as a function of the time.

5. The retarding effect of fluid friction on a rotating disk is proportional to its angular velocity. If the disk starts with a velocity of 100 revolutions per minute and revolves 60 times during the first minute, find its velocity as a function of the time.

6. According to Newton's law the rate at which a substance cools in air is proportional to the difference of its temperature and that of the air. If the temperature of the air is 20° C. and the substance cools from 100° to 60° in 20 min., when will its temperature become 30°?

7. A substance is undergoing transformation into another at a rate proportional to the amount of the substance remaining untransformed. If that amount is 31.4 at the end of 1 hr. and 9.7 at the end of 3 hrs., find the amount at the start and find how many hours will elapse before only 1% will remain.

8. When a liquid rotates about a vertical axis, show that its surface forms a paraboloid of revolution. Observe that the weight of a particle of water at the surface and its centrifugal force must have as resultant a force perpendicular to the surface.

9. Through each point of a curve lines are drawn parallel to the axes to form a rectangle two of whose sides lie on the axes. Find the curve which cuts every rectangle of this kind into two areas one of which is twice the other.

10. Find the surface of a mirror such that all light from a fixed point is reflected parallel to a fixed line. Take the fixed point as origin and let the light be reflected parallel to the x-axis. Use the polar coördinate r and the x-coördinate as variables.

11. In a certain type of reflecting telescope light converging toward a fixed point is reflected by a mirror to another point. Find the shape of the mirror.

12. If a man can earn 5 dollars per day over expenses and keep his earnings continuously invested at 6% compound interest, how long will it take to save $25,000?

13. If a man can earn s dollars per year over expenses and keep his savings continuously invested at 6% compound interest, how long will be needed to obtain an income of s dollars per year from investments?

14. The amount an elastic string of natural length l stretches under a force F is klF, k being constant. Find the amount it stretches when suspended from one end and allowed to stretch under its own weight w.

15. Find the amount the string of the preceding problem stretches if it is hung up with a weight P attached to the lower end.

16. Consider a vertical column of air and assume that the pressure at any level is due to the weight of air above. Find the pressure as a function of the height if the pressure at sea level is 14.7 lbs. per sq. in., and at an elevation of 1600 ft. is 13.8 lbs. per sq. in. Assume Boyle's law that the density of the gas is proportional to the pressure.

17. If air in moving from one level to another expands without receiving or giving out heat, that is, adiabatically,

$$p = k\rho^n,$$

where p is the pressure, ρ the density, and k, n constants. Assuming adiabatical expansion, if the density at sea level is .08 lbs. per cu. ft. and the pressure 2100 lbs. per sq. ft., find the height of the atmosphere.

18. If the coefficient of friction between a belt and pulley is μ and the angle of lapping α, show that the tensions T_1, T_2 in the two sides of the belt when it is slipping satisfy the equation

$$T_2 = T_1 e^{\mu\alpha}.$$

19. If the velocity is high centrifugal force reduces the pressure of the belt upon the pulley. Assuming the weight of the belt to be w lbs. per unit length and its velocity v, find the equation connecting the tensions in the two sides of the belts.

20. The end of a vertical shaft of radius a is supported by a flat-step bearing. If the horizontal surface of the bearing carries a uniform load of p lbs per sq. in. (new bearing) and the coefficient of friction is μ, find the work done against friction in one revolution.

An old bearing is worn a little more at the edge than at the center. Ultimately the pressure varies in such a way that the wear is the same at all points. Assuming that the wear at any point is proportional to the work of friction per unit area at that point, find the law of variation of pressure and show that with a given total load the work per revolution is only $\frac{3}{4}$ that in a new bearing.

21. Assuming that the density of sea water under a pressure of p lbs. per sq. in. is

$$1 + 0.000003 \, p$$

times its density at the surface, show that the surface of an ocean 5 miles deep is about 450 ft. lower than it would be if water were incompressible.

22. A cylindrical tank with vertical axis is 6 ft. deep and 4 ft. in diameter. If the tank is full of water, find the time required to empty through a 2-inch hole at the bottom.

23. Find the time of emptying if the axis of the tank in the preceding problem is horizontal.

24. Two vertical tanks each 4 ft. deep and 4 ft. in diameter are connected by a short 2-inch pipe at the bottom. If one of the tanks is full and the other empty, find the time required to reach the same level in both. Assume that the velocity through the pipe is the same as that through an orifice under the same effective pressure.

25. Into a tank of square cross-section, 4 ft. deep and 6 ft. in diameter water flows at the rate of 10 cu. ft. per minute. Find the time required to fill the tank if at the same time the water leaks out through an inch hole at the bottom.

26. If half the water runs out of a conical funnel in 2 min., find the time required to empty.

27. A vertical tank has a slight leak at the bottom. Assuming that the water escapes at a rate proportional to the pressure and that $\frac{1}{10}$ of it escapes the first day, find the time required to half empty.

28. In a tank are 100 gals. of brine containing 50 lbs. of dissolved salt. Water runs into the tank at the rate of 3 gals. per min., and the mixture runs out at the rate of 2 gals. per min., the concentration being kept uniform by stirring. How much salt is in the tank at the end of one hour?

29. Suppose the bottom of the tank in the preceding problem is covered with a mixture of salt and insoluble material. Assume that the salt dissolves at a rate proportional to the difference between the concentration of the solution and that of a saturated solution (3 lbs. salt per gal.) and that if the water were fresh 1 lb. salt would dissolve per minute. How much salt will be in the solution at the end of one hour?

30. Oxygen flows through one tube into a liter flask filled with air and the mixture of oxygen and air escapes through another. If the action is so slow that the mixture in the flask may be considered uniform, what percentage of oxygen will the flask contain after 5 liters have passed through? Assume that air contains 21% oxygen.

31. The air in a recently used class-room $30' \times 30' \times 12'$ tested 0.12% carbon dioxide. How many cu. ft. air containing 0.04% CO_2 must be admitted per minute that 10 minutes later it may test 0.06% CO_2.

32. If the average person breathes 18 times per minute exhaling each time 100 cu. in. containing 4% CO_2, find the per cent CO_2 in the air of a class-room $\frac{1}{2}$ hour after a class of 50 enters, assuming the air fresh at the start and that the ventilators admit 1000 cu. ft. fresh air per minute. Let the volume of the room be 10,000 cu. ft. and assume that fresh air contains 0.04% CO_2.

33. A factory $200' \times 45' \times 12'$ receives through the ventilators 10,000 cu. ft. fresh air per minute containing 0.04% CO_2. A half hour after the help enters at 7 A.M. the CO_2 content has risen to 0.12%. What value is to be anticipated at noon?

34. A brick wall ($k = 0.0015$) is 30 cm. thick. If the inner surface is at 20° C. and the outer at 0° C., find the temperature in the wall as a function of the distance from the outer surface. Also find the heat loss per day through a square meter.

35. A steam pipe 20 cm. in diameter is protected with a covering 10 cm. thick of magnesia ($k = 0.00017$). If the outer surface is at 30° C. and the surface of the pipe 160° C., determine the temperature in the covering as a function of the distance from the center of the pipe. Also determine the heat loss per day through a meter length of the pipe.

36. A wire whose resistance per cm. length is 0.1 ohm is imbedded along the axis of a cylindrical cement tube of radii 0.5 cm. and 1.0 cm. An electric current of 5 amp. is found to keep a temperature difference of 125° C. between the inner and outer surfaces. What is the conductivity of the cement?

37. The amount of light absorbed in passing through a thin sheet of water is proportional to the amount falling on the surface and also proportional to the thickness of the sheet. If one-half the light were absorbed in penetrating 10 ft., how much would reach the depth of 100 ft.?

38. A porous material dries in a confined space at a rate proportional to its moisture content and also to the difference between the moisture content of air and that of saturated air. A quantity of material containing 10 lbs. of moisture was placed in a closed storeroom of volume 2000 cu. ft. The air at the beginning had a humidity of 25%. Saturated air at the given temperature contains approximately 0.015 lbs. moisture per cu. ft. If the material lost half its moisture the first day, estimate its condition at the end of the second day.

39. How long would be needed for the substance of the preceding problem to lose 90% of its moisture if the humidity of air is kept at 25% by ventilation.

40. A mass of insoluble material contains 30 lbs. of salt in its pores. The mass is agitated with 30 gals. of water for 1 hour when one-half the salt is found to be dissolved. How much would have dissolved in the same time if we had used double the amount of water? Assume the rate of solution proportional to the amount of undissolved salt and also proportional to the difference between the concentration of the solution and that of a saturated solution (3 lbs. salt per gal.).

41. A mass of inert material containing 5 lbs. of salt in its pores is agitated with 10 gals. of water. In 5 minutes 2 lbs. of salt have dissolved. When will the salt be 99% dissolved?

CHAPTER II

OTHER FIRST ORDER EQUATIONS

11. Exact Differential Equations. — The equation

$$M \, dx + N \, dy = 0 \tag{11a}$$

is called exact if their exists a function u with total differential

$$du = M \, dx + N \, dy. \tag{11b}$$

In this case (11a) can be written

$$du = 0$$

and so its solution is

$$u = c.$$

It is shown in calculus that $M \, dx + N \, dy$ is an exact differential when and only when

$$\frac{\partial M}{\partial x} = \frac{\partial N}{\partial y}. \tag{11c}$$

To determine whether an equation is exact we therefore calculate these partial derivatives and observe whether they are equal.

To solve the equation it is necessary to find the function u whose differential is $M \, dx + N \, dy$. The terms can often be arranged in groups each of which is an exact differential. The value of u is then obtained by integrating these groups separately.

If this cannot be done, the solution oan be determined from the fact that

$$\frac{\partial u}{\partial x} = M.$$

By integrating with y constant, we get

$$u = \int M \, dx + f(y),$$

the constant of integration being possibly a function of y. This function of y can be found by equating the differential of u to $N \, dx + N \, dy$. Since $df(y)$ gives terms containing y only, *f (y) can usually be found by integrating the terms in N dy that do not contain x.* In exceptional cases this may not give the correct result. The answer should therefore be tested by differentiation.

Example 1. $(x + y) \, dx + (2y + x) \, dy = 0$. This equation can be written

$$x \, dx + 2y \, dy + (y \, dx + x \, dy) = 0.$$

It is therefore exact and its solution is

$$x^2 + 2y^2 + 2xy = c.$$

Example 2. $e^y \, dx + (xe^y - 2y) \, dy = 0$.
In this case

$$\frac{\partial M}{\partial y} = \frac{\partial}{\partial y}(e^y) = e^y,$$

$$\frac{\partial N}{\partial x} = \frac{\partial}{\partial x}(xe^y - 2y) = e^y.$$

These derivatives being equal, the equation is exact. Hence

$$u = \int e^y \, dx = xe^y + f(y),$$

$$du = e^y \, dx + \left[xe^y + f'(y)\right] dy,$$

where $f'(y)$ is the derivative of $f(y)$. Comparing with the original equation, we see that

$$f'(y) = -2y$$

and so

$$f(y) = -y^2.$$

The solution is

$$xe^y - y^2 = c.$$

The value of $f(y)$ could have been obtained by integrating $-2\,y\,dy$ which is the part of

$$(xe^y - 2\,y)\,dy$$

not containing x.

12. Integrating Factors. — If an equation of the form

$$M\,dx + N\,dy = 0$$

is not exact it can always be made exact by multiplying by a proper factor. Such a multiplier is called an *integrating factor*.

For example, the equation

$$y\,(1 + xy)\,dx - x\,dy = 0$$

is not exact. It can however be written

$$y\,dx - x\,dy + xy^2\,dx = 0.$$

Dividing by y^2,

$$\frac{y\,dx - x\,dy}{y^2} + x\,dx = 0.$$

Both terms of this equation are exact differentials. The solution is

$$\frac{x}{y} + \frac{1}{2}x^2 = c.$$

An integrating factor in this case is $\dfrac{1}{y^2}$.

While an equation of the form $M\,dx + N\,dy = 0$ always has integrating factors, there is no general method of finding them.

13. Linear Equations. — A differential equation of the form

$$\frac{ay}{dx} + Py = Q, \tag{13a}$$

where P and Q are functions of x or constants, is called *linear*. A linear equation is thus one of the first degree in one of the variables (y in this case) and its derivative. Any functions of the other variable may occur.

When the equation is written in the form (13a),

$$e^{\int P\,dx}$$

is an integrating factor; for, when multiplied by this factor, the equation becomes

$$e^{\int P\,dx}\frac{dy}{dx} + ye^{\int P\,dx}P = e^{\int P\,dx}Q.$$

The left side is the derivative of

$$ye^{\int P\,dx}.$$

Hence

$$ye^{\int P\,dx} = \int e^{\int P\,dx}Q\,dx + c \qquad (13b)$$

is the solution.

Example 1. $\dfrac{dy}{dx} + \dfrac{2}{x}y = x^3.$

In this case

$$\int P\,dx = \int \frac{2}{x}\,dx = 2\ln x = \ln x^2.$$

Hence

$$e^{\int P\,dx} = e^{\ln x^2} = x^2.$$

The integrating factor is therefore x^2. Multiplying by x^2 and changing to differentials, the equation becomes

$$x^2\,dy + 2\,xy\,dx = x^5\,dx.$$

The solution is

$$x^2 y = \frac{1}{6} x^6 + c.$$

Example 2. $(1 + y^2) \, dx - (xy + y + y^3) \, dy = 0.$

This is an equation of the first degree in x and dx. Dividing by $(1 + y^2) \, dy$, it becomes

$$\frac{dx}{dy} - \frac{y}{1 + y^2} x = y.$$

P is here a function of y and

$$\int P \, dy = \int \frac{-y \, dy}{1 + y^2} = -\frac{1}{2} \ln (1 + y^2),$$

$$e^{\int P \, dy} = \frac{1}{\sqrt{1 + y^2}}.$$

multiplying by this factor, the equation becomes

$$\frac{dx}{\sqrt{1 + y^2}} - \frac{xy \, dy}{(1 + y^2)^{\frac{3}{2}}} = \frac{y \, dy}{\sqrt{1 + y^2}},$$

whence

$$\frac{x}{\sqrt{1 + y^2}} = \sqrt{1 + y^2} + c,$$

and

$$x = 1 + y^2 + c \sqrt{1 + y^2}.$$

14. Equations Reducible to Linear Form. — An equation of the form

$$\frac{dy}{dx} + Py = Qy^n \tag{14}$$

where P and Q are functions of x can be made linear by a change of variable.   Dividing by y^n it becomes

$$y^{-n} \frac{dy}{dx} + Py^{-n+1} = Q.$$

If we take

$$y^{-n} = u$$

as new variable the equation becomes

$$\frac{1}{1-n}\frac{du}{dx} + Pu = Q,$$

which is linear.

Example. $\dfrac{dy}{dx} + \dfrac{2}{x}y = \dfrac{y^3}{x^3}.$

Division by y^3 gives

$$y^{-3}\frac{dy}{dx} + \frac{2}{x}y^{-2} = \frac{1}{x^3}.$$

Let

$$u = y^{-2}.$$

Then

$$\frac{du}{dx} = -2\,y^{-3}\frac{dy}{dx},$$

whence

$$y^{-3}\frac{dy}{dx} = -\frac{1}{2}\frac{du}{dx}.$$

Substituting tnese values we get

$$-\frac{1}{2}\frac{du}{dx} + \frac{2}{x}u = \frac{1}{x^3}$$

and so

$$\frac{du}{dx} - \frac{4}{x}u = -\frac{2}{x^3}.$$

This is a linear equation with solution

$$u = \frac{1}{3\,x^2} + cx^4,$$

or, since $u = y^{-2}$,

$$\frac{1}{y^2} = \frac{1}{3\,x^2} + cx^4.$$

15. Homogeneous Equations. — A function $f(x, y)$ is said to be a homogeneous equation of the nth degree if

$$f(tx, ty) = t^n f(x, y).$$

Thus, $\sqrt{x^2 + y^2}$ is a homogeneous function of the first degree; for

$$\sqrt{x^2 t^2 + y^2 t^2} = t \sqrt{x^2 + y^2}.$$

It is easily seen that a polynomial all of whose terms are of the nth degree is a homogeneous function of the nth degree.

The differential equation

$$M \, dx + N \, dy = 0$$

is called homogeneous if M and N are homogeneous functions of the same degree. To solve a homogeneous equation, substitute

$$y = vx,$$

or

$$x = vy.$$

The new equation will be separable.

Example 1. $x \dfrac{dy}{dx} - y = \sqrt{x^2 + y^2}.$

This is a homogeneous equation of the first degree. Substituting $y = vx$, it becomes

$$x \left(v + x \frac{dv}{dx} \right) - vx = \sqrt{x^2 + v^2 x^2},$$

whence

$$x \frac{dv}{dx} = \sqrt{1 + v^2}.$$

This is a separable equation with solution

$$x = c \, (v + \sqrt{1 + v^2}).$$

Replacing v by $\frac{y}{x}$, transposing, squaring, etc.,

$$x^2 - 2\,cy = c^2.$$

Example 2. $y\left(\dfrac{dy}{dx}\right)^2 + 2\,x\dfrac{dy}{dx} - y = 0.$

Solving for $\dfrac{dy}{dx}$, we get

$$\frac{dy}{dx} = \frac{-x \pm \sqrt{x^2 + y^2}}{y},$$

whence

$$y\,dy + x\,dx = \pm\sqrt{x^2 + y^2}\,dx.$$

This is a homogeneous equation of the first degree. It is however much easier to divide by $\sqrt{x^2 + y^2}$ and integrate at once. The result is

$$\frac{x\,dx + y\,dy}{\sqrt{x^2 + y^2}} = \pm\,dx.$$

Integration gives

$$\sqrt{x^2 + y^2} = c \pm x$$

and so

$$y^2 = c^2 \pm 2\,cx.$$

Since c may be either positive or negative, the answer is equivalent to

$$y^2 = c^2 + 2\,cx.$$

16. Change of Variable. — We have solved the homogeneous equation by taking

$$v = \frac{y}{x}$$

as new variable. It may be possible to reduce any equation to a simpler form by taking some function u of x and y as new variable or by taking two functions u and v as new variables.

If the differential equation only is known some expression appearing in the equation may be a good variable. Thus it often happens that y appears only in the combinations y^2 and $y \frac{dy}{dx}$. By taking

$$y^2 = u, \quad y \frac{dy}{dx} = \frac{1}{2} \frac{du}{dx},$$

a simpler equation is obtained.

If the equation is obtained in the solution of a problem, any quantity which plays a prominent role in the statement of the problem may be a good variable. Thus, in solving the reflector problem (Art. 6) we used as variables the distances from the two points which were directly suggested by the problem itself.

Example. $(x - y)^2 \frac{dy}{dx} = a^2.$

. Let $x - y = u.$ Then

$$1 - \frac{dy}{dx} = \frac{du}{dx}$$

and the differential equation becomes

$$u^2 \left(1 - \frac{du}{dx} \right) = a^2,$$

$$u^2 - a^2 = u^2 \frac{du}{dx}.$$

The variables are separable. The solution is

$$x = u + \frac{a}{2} \ln \frac{u - a}{u + a} + c$$

$$= x - y + \frac{a}{2} \ln \left(\frac{x - y - a}{x - y + a} \right) + c,$$

whence

$$y = \frac{a}{2} \ln \frac{x - y - a}{x - y + a} + c.$$

17. Simultaneous Equations. — We often have two differential equations

$$\frac{dx}{dt} = f_1(x, y), \frac{dy}{dt} = f_2(x, y),$$

containing two dependent variables x and y and their derivatives with respect to the same independent variable t. It may be possible to combine the equations algebraically so as to get an equation containing only one dependent variable, which may be x or y or any function of x and y. We solve for this and substitute in one of the original equations to complete the solution.

Example 1. $\frac{dx}{dt} = k_1(x - y), \frac{dy}{dt} = k_2 y.$

The second equation contains only one dependent variable y. Its solution is

$$y = c_1 e^{k_2 t}.$$

Substituting this value in the first equation,

$$\frac{dx}{dt} - k_1 x = - k_1 c_1 e^{k_2 t}.$$

This is a linear equation with solution

$$x = c_2 e^{k_1 t} - \frac{k_1 c_1}{k_2 - k_1} e^{k_2 t}.$$

Example 2. $\frac{dy}{dt} = x - y, \quad \frac{dx}{dt} = 2 y.$

Multiplying the first equation by a constant a, the second by b and adding, we get

$$\frac{d}{dt}(ay + bx) = ax + (2b - a)y.$$

The right side of this equation will be a multiple of the expression in parentheses if

$$\frac{a}{b} = \frac{2b - a}{a}.$$

A solution of this is

$$a = b = 1,$$

and so

$$\frac{d}{dt}(y + x) = x + y.$$

Solving for $x + y$,

$$x + y = c_1 e^t.$$

Substituting

$$x = c_1 e^t - y \qquad\qquad (17)$$

in the first equation we get

$$\frac{dy}{dt} + 2\,y = c_1 e^t.$$

This is a linear equation with solution

$$y = c_2 e^{-2t} + \frac{1}{3} c_1 e^t.$$

Substituting in (17), we get

$$x = \frac{2}{3} c_1 e^t - c_2 e^{-2t}.$$

EXERCISES

Solve the following differential equations:

1. $(3\,x^2 + 2\,xy - y^2)\,dx + (x^2 - 2\,xy - 3\,y^2)\,dy = 0.$
2. $x\dfrac{dy}{dx} + y = x^2.$
3. $(x^2 + y^2)\,dx + 2\,xy\,dy = 0.$
4. $(x^2 + y^2)\,dx - 2\,xy\,dy = 0.$
5. $y\,dx + (x + y)\,dy = 0.$
6. $y\,dx - (x + y)\,dy = 0.$
7. $x\,dy + y\,dx = y^2\,dx.$
8. $\dfrac{dy}{dx} - ay = e^{bx}.$

9. $x^2 \dfrac{dy}{dx} - 2\,xy = 3.$

10. $x^2 \dfrac{dy}{dx} - 2\,xy = 3\,y.$

11. $(2\,xy^2 - y)\,dx + x\,dy = 0.$

12. $\tan x \dfrac{dy}{dx} - y = a.$

13. $(x^2 - 1)^{\frac{3}{2}}\,dy + (x^3 + 3\,xy\,\sqrt{x^2 - 1})\,dx = 0.$

14. $ye^v\,dx = (y^3 + 2\,xe^v)\,dy.$

15. $(xy\,e^{\frac{x}{v}} + y^2)\,dx - x^2 e^{\frac{x}{v}}\,dy = 0.$

16. $\dfrac{dy}{dx} + y = xy^3.$

17. $x \dfrac{dy}{dx} - 3\,y + x^4\,y^2 = 0.$

18. $x\,dx + y\,dy = x\,dy - y\,dx.$

19. $(xy^2 - x)\,dx + (y + xy)\,dy = 0.$

20. $x\,dy - y\,dx = \sqrt{x^2 + y^2}\,dx.$

21. $(\sin x + y)\,dy + (y\cos x - x^2)\,dx = 0.$

22. $x\,dy - y\,dx = x\,\sqrt{x^2 + y^2}\,dx.$

23. $(1 + x^2)\,dy + (xy - x^2)\,dx = 0.$

24. $y\,dx = (y^3 - x)\,dy.$

25. $y \dfrac{dy}{dx} + y^2\cot x = \cos x.$

26. $(x + y - 1)\,dx + (2\,x + 2\,y - 3)\,dy = 0.$

27. $3\,y^2 \dfrac{dy}{dx} - y^3 = x.$

28. $x \left(\dfrac{dy}{dx}\right)^2 - 2\,y \dfrac{dy}{dx} - x = 0.$

29. $\left(\dfrac{dy}{dx}\right)^2 - (x + y) \dfrac{dy}{dx} + xy = 0.$

30. $e^v \left(\dfrac{dy}{dx} + 1\right) = e^x.$

31. $(2\,x + 3\,y - 1)\,dx + (4\,x + 6\,y - 5)\,dy = 0.$

32. $(3\,y^2 + 3\,xy + x^2)\,dx = (x^2 + 2\,xy)\,dy.$

33. $\dfrac{dx}{dt} + x = e^t, \qquad \dfrac{dy}{dt} = x.$

34. $\dfrac{dy}{dt} + x = 1, \qquad \dfrac{dx}{dt} + y = 1.$

35. $\dfrac{dx}{dt} = x - 2\,y, \quad 6\dfrac{dy}{dt} = x - y.$

36. $4\dfrac{dx}{dt} - \dfrac{dy}{dt} + 3\,x = \sin t, \qquad \dfrac{dx}{dt} + y = \cos t.$

PROBLEMS

1. Using rectangular coördinates, find the shape of a reflector such that light coming from a fixed point is reflected parallel to a fixed line.

2. In Example 1, Art. 8, suppose the outflow passes through a second 100 gal. tank initially filled with pure water. How much salt will this tank contain at the end of 1 hour?

3. If i is the current, the electromotive force across a resistance R is Ri and that across an inductance L is $L \frac{di}{dt}$. The e.m.f. impressed upon a circuit containing a resistance R and an inductance L in series is

$$e = E \sin (\omega t),$$

E and ω being constants. Find the current at time t if $i = 0$ when $t = 0$.

4. Two circuits of resistance R_1, R_2 and inductance L_1, L_2 respectively are connected in parallel between the mains of a transmission line. If the total current they receive is

$$i = I \sin (\omega t),$$

find the current in each circuit and the e.m.f. between the mains assuming that both currents are zero when $t = 0$.

5. A cylinder containing gas is rotated with constant angular velocity ω about its axis. Ultimately the mass of gas will rotate like a rigid body. Assuming Boyle's law and taking account of centrifugal force, find the law connecting the pressure of the gas and the distance from the axis. Would a similar law be obtained, if instead of a cylinder, the container had any other shape?

6. In a chemical reaction a substance c decomposes into two substances x and y, the rate at which these products are formed being proportional to the amount of c present. If at the beginning $c = 1$, $x = 0$, $y = 0$, and at the end of 1 hr. $c = \frac{1}{2}$, $x = \frac{1}{8}$, $y = \frac{3}{8}$, find x and y as functions of the time.

7. In a certain chemical reaction, 1 mol. of y is produced for each mol. of x consumed, the rate being proportional to the amount of x present, and at the same time y by a reverse reaction is converted into x at a rate proportional to the amount of y present. Chemical analysis showed

$$\begin{array}{cccc} t = 0, & 3, & \infty \\ x = 10, & 6, & 5.5 \\ y = 0, & 4, & 4.5. \end{array}$$

Find x and y as functions of t.

8. Radioactive substances are transformed at a rate proportional to the amount of substance present. Through the decomposition of a mol. of *Ra B* a mol of *Ra C* is produced, the rate being such that $\frac{1}{2}$ the *Ra B* disappears in 27 minutes. Similarly the *Ra C* decomposes at a rate such that $\frac{1}{2}$ of it is lost in 19.5 min. If initially 1 mol. of *Ra B* is present, find the amount of *Ra B* and *Ra C* at the end of 1 hr.

9. When light passes from a medium of refractive index μ to one of index μ',

$$\frac{\mu'}{\mu} = \frac{\sin \theta}{\sin \theta'},$$

θ and θ' being the angles which the incident and refracted ray make with the normal to the surface of separation. According to Einstein's theory, the gravitational field of the sun deflects a ray of light as if it had a refractive index.

$$\mu = 1 + \frac{a}{r},$$

where a is constant and r the distance from the center of the sun. Find the path described by the ray.

10. Suppose bacteria grow at a rate proportional to the number present but that they produce toxines which destroy them at a rate proportional to the number of bacteria and to the amount of toxin. Suppose further that the rate of production of toxin is proportional to the number of bacteria. Show that the number increases to a maximum and then decreases to zero and at time t is given by

$$N = \frac{4 M}{(e^{kt} + e^{-kt})^2}$$

where M is the maximum number and t is measured from the time when the number is a maximum.

CHAPTER III

SPECIAL TYPES OF SECOND ORDER EQUATIONS

18. Equations Immediately Integrable. — An equation of the form

$$\frac{d^2y}{dx^2} = f(x) \tag{18}$$

can be solved directly by two integrations. The first integration gives

$$\frac{dy}{dx} = \int f(x)\, dx + c_1.$$

A second integration gives the general solution in the form

$$y = \int \left(\int f(x)\, dx \right) dx + c_1 x + c_2.$$

19. Equations not Containing y. — An equation not containing y can be solved for the second derivative and so reduced to the form

$$\frac{d^2y}{dx^2} = f\left(x, \frac{dy}{dx} \right). \tag{19a}$$

Take as new variable

$$p = \frac{dy}{dx}. \tag{19b}$$

Then

$$\frac{d^2y}{dx^2} = \frac{dp}{dx}$$

and so (19a) can be written

$$\frac{dp}{dx} = f(x, p).$$

This is a first order equation whose solution has the form

$$p = F(x, c_1),$$

where c_1 is the constant of integration.

Substituting $\dfrac{dy}{dx}$ for p, we have

$$\frac{dy}{dx} = F(x, c_1),$$

whence

$$y = \int F(x, c_1)\, dx + c_2.$$

Example. $(1 + x)\dfrac{d^2y}{dx^2} + \dfrac{dy}{dx} = 0.$

Substituting p for $\dfrac{dy}{dx}$ we have

$$(1 + x)\frac{dp}{dx} + p = 0.$$

This is an exact equation with solution

$$(1 + x)p = c_1.$$

Replacing p by $\dfrac{dy}{dx}$ and separating the variables, we have

$$dy = \frac{c_1\, dx}{1 + x},$$

whence

$$y = c_1 \ln(1 + x) + c_2.$$

20. Equations not Containing x. — An equation not containing x can be reduced to the form

$$\frac{d^2y}{dx^2} = f(y, p). \tag{20a}$$

Substitute

$$\frac{dy}{dx} = p \tag{20b}$$

and write the second derivative in the form

$$\frac{d^2y}{dx^2} = \frac{dp}{dx} = \frac{dp}{dy}\frac{dy}{dx} = p\frac{dp}{dy}. \tag{20c}$$

These substitutions bring (20a) to the form

$$p\frac{dp}{dy} = f(y, p).$$

This is a first order equation which can be solved for p. Replacing p by $\frac{dy}{dx}$ the result is a first order equation which can be solved by a separation of the variables.

Example. $y\frac{d^2y}{dx^2} = y^2\frac{dy}{dx} + \left(\frac{dy}{dx}\right)^2.$

Substituting

$$\frac{dy}{dx} = p, \qquad\qquad \frac{d^2y}{dx^2} = p\frac{dp}{dy}$$

the equation becomes

$$yp\frac{dp}{dy} = y^2p + p^2.$$

Dividing by p,

$$y\frac{dp}{dy} = y^2 + p.$$

The solution of this equation is

$$\frac{p}{y} = y + c_1,$$

whence

$$\frac{dy}{dx} = y(y + c_1)$$

and

$$x = \int \frac{dy}{y(y + c_1)} = \frac{1}{c_1}\ln\frac{y}{y + c_1} + c_2. \tag{20d}$$

In solving this problem we divided both sides of the equation by p. This is allowable since

$$p = 0$$

gives

$$y = c \tag{20e}$$

a solution which contains only one constant of integration whereas we are determining the general solution with two constants of integration. It is to be noted that (20d) is a solution of the original differential equation and that it cannot be obtained by giving special values to the constants in (20c). Such a solution is called *singular* and in some problems might be important.

EXERCISES

Solve the following differential equations:

1. $x \dfrac{d^2y}{dx^2} = 1 + x^2.$

2. $x \dfrac{d^2y}{dx^2} + \dfrac{dy}{dx} + x = 0.$

3. $\dfrac{d^2y}{dx^2} = x + a.$

4. $\dfrac{d^2y}{dx^2} = y.$

5. $\dfrac{d^2y}{dx^2} + k^2 y = 0.$

6. $\dfrac{d^2s}{dt^2} = -\dfrac{k^2}{s^2}.$

7. $\dfrac{d^2s}{dt^2} + a^2 \left(\dfrac{ds}{dt}\right)^2 = b^2.$

8. $x \dfrac{d^2y}{dx^2} = \sqrt{1 + \left(\dfrac{dy}{dx}\right)^2}.$

9. $(x+1) \dfrac{d^2y}{dx^2} - (x+2) \dfrac{dy}{dx} + x + 2 = 0.$

10. $y \dfrac{d^2y}{dx^2} = 1 + \left(\dfrac{dy}{dx}\right)^2.$

11. $x^2 \dfrac{d^2y}{dx^2} + x \dfrac{dy}{dx} = 1.$

12. $\dfrac{d^2s}{dt^2} = \dfrac{a^2}{s^3}.$

21. Deflection of Beams. — When a beam is bent by vertical forces as shown in Fig. 21a, the fibers in the upper part are stretched and those in the lower part compressed. There is then a neutral curve AB along which they are neither stretched nor compressed. It is seen from the figure that the amount ds a fiber of natural length s is stretched or compressed is given by the equation

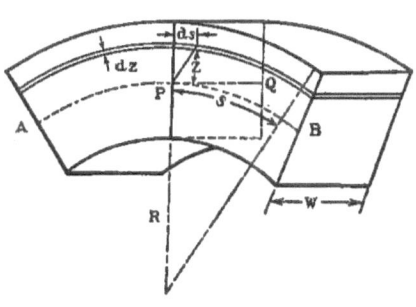

$$\frac{ds}{z} = \frac{s}{R},$$

where z is its distance from the neutral curve and R is the radius of the circle in which the neutral curve is bent.

Fig. 21a.

By Hooke's law the tension in the fibers between z and $z + dz$ is

$$T = Ew\, dz \cdot \frac{ds}{s} = Ew\, dz \cdot \frac{z}{R},$$

where E is the stretch modulus of elasticity of the material and w the width of the beam. Since there is no resultant force along the beam

$$\int Ew\, dz \cdot \frac{z}{R} = \frac{E}{R} \int wz\, dz = 0$$

showing that the neutral curve passes through the center of gravity of each cross section. The moment of the total stress about an axis PQ perpendicular to the beam is

$$M = \frac{E}{R} \int wz^2\, dz = \frac{EI}{R} \tag{21a}$$

when I is the moment of inertia of the section area about that axis.

Let (x, y) be the coördinates of P, x being measured

along the beam. Since the curvature is usually very small, the slope $\dfrac{dy}{dx}$ is nearly zero and so

$$\frac{1}{R} = \frac{\dfrac{d^2y}{dx^2}}{\left[1 + \left(\dfrac{dy}{dx}\right)^2\right]^{\frac{3}{2}}} = \frac{d^2y}{dx^2}$$

approximately. Hence (21a) can be written

$$EI\frac{d^2y}{dx^2} = M. \tag{21b}$$

M, called the bending moment, is the moment about P of all forces *on one side* of P, those acting upward producing positive moments, those downward negative. To find the curve in which a beam bends we determine M as a function of x and solve the differential equation (21b). In the problems considered here the beam is of uniform material and has a constant

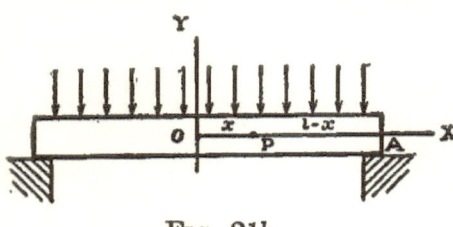

Fig. 21b.

cross section. Hence E and I are constants.

Example. Find the deflection of a beam of length $2\,l$, supported at its ends and loaded with a weight w per unit length.

Take the origin at the center of the beam. The total weight supported being $2\,lw$, the upward thrust of the support at each end is lw. Consider forces on the right of the point P. At the end is an upward thrust lw. Its moment about P is

$$wl\,(l - x).$$

The only other force on the section PA is the load $w\,(l - x)$ between P and A. Since the load is uniformly distributed, this can be considered as acting through its center of gravity at distance $\frac{1}{2}\,(l - x)$ from P. Its moment is then

$$- w\,(l - x) \cdot \tfrac{1}{2}\,(l - x),$$

the negative sign being used because the force is downward. The total moment about P is

$$M = wl\,(l - x) - \frac{w}{2}\,(l - x)^2 = \tfrac{1}{2}\,w\,(l^2 - x^2).$$

The differential equation is therefore

$$EI\,\frac{d^2y}{dx^2} = \tfrac{1}{2}\,w\,(l^2 - x^2).$$

A first integration gives

$$EI\,\frac{dy}{dx} = \tfrac{1}{2}\,w\left(l^2 x - \frac{x^3}{3}\right) + c_1.$$

Since the beam is horizontal at the center

$$x = 0, \qquad \frac{dy}{dx} = 0$$

and so $c_1 = 0$.   A second integration gives

$$EI\,y = \tfrac{1}{2}\,w\left(\frac{l^2 x^2}{2} - \frac{x^4}{12}\right) + c_2.$$

Since we have taken the origin on the curve $c_2 = 0$.   The equation of the elastic curve is therefore

$$EI\,y = \tfrac{1}{2}\,w\left(\frac{l^2 x^2}{2} - \frac{x^4}{12}\right).$$

The maximum departure of the beam from a straight line is

$$y = \frac{5\,wl^4}{24}$$

at the end, given by placing $x = l$. This is ordinarily called the *deflection* of the beam.

22. Equilibrium of a Cable. — Let ABC (Fig. 22) be a perfectly flexible cable fastened at A and C and loaded in any way. Take the x-axis horizontal and the y-axis through the lowest point B on the curve. Consider the part of the cable between B and the variable point $P\,(x, y)$ on the curve. This is in equilibrium under the action of three forces:

(1) A horizontal tension H at B exerted by the section AB of the cable.

(2) A tension T along the tangent at P due to the part PC of the cable.

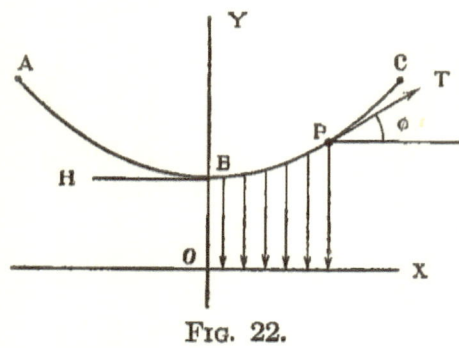

Fig. 22.

(3) A downward force equal to the load W on the part BP of the cable.

The total component of force toward the right must equal that toward the left, and the component of force acting upward must equal that acting downward.

Hence

$$T \cos \phi = H,$$
$$T \sin \phi = W. \qquad (22a)$$

Dividing the second equation by the first, we get

$$\tan \phi = \frac{dy}{dx} = \frac{W}{H}. \qquad (22b)$$

Since H is constant, if W is a known function of x, this can be integrated at once. In some cases W is not known but its derivative can be easily determined. In that case, differentiation gives

$$\frac{d^2y}{dx^2} = \frac{1}{H}\frac{dW}{dx} \qquad (22c)$$

from which we can determine the equation of the curve.

The answer contains the constant H. This can be determined by substituting the known coördinates of B and the ends of the cable.

23. Motion of a Particle in a Straight Line. — If F is the resultant of all forces acting on a particle of mass m, its acceleration a is given by the equation

$$F = m\,a. \qquad (23a)$$

If the particle moves along a straight line and s is its distance from a fixed point of the line, its velocity is

$$v = \frac{ds}{dt}, \tag{23b}$$

and its acceleration is

$$a = \frac{dv}{dt} = \frac{d^2s}{dt^2}. \tag{23c}$$

In using these formulas we can measure s in either direction along the line but must then consider as positive the direction in which s increases. The quantities F, v, and a are positive or negative according as they point in the positive or negative direction thus defined.

Example. When a body sinks slowly in a liquid the resistance is approximately proportional to the velocity. If the particle starts from rest, find its motion.

Let s, considered positive downward, be the distance the body sinks in t seconds. If m is its mass and g the acceleration of gravity, the force of gravity is

$$mg,$$

which is positive since the force is downward. The resistance acting upward and being proportional to the velocity is

$$- kv.$$

The total force acting on the body is then

$$F = mg - kv.$$

Hence equation (23a) is

$$mg - kv = ma = m\frac{dv}{dt}.$$

Separating the variables and integrating, we get

$$\ln (mg - kv) = -\frac{k}{m}t + c$$

Since $v = 0$ when $t = 0$

$$\ln (mg) = c.$$

Subtracting from the preceding equation and solving for $mg - kv$,

$$mg - kv = mg\, e^{-\frac{k}{m}t}.$$

Since $v = \dfrac{ds}{dt}$, integration gives

$$mg\, t - ks = -\frac{m^2 g}{k} e^{-\frac{k}{m}t} + c.$$

Since $s = 0$ when $t = 0$,

$$c = \frac{m^2 g}{k}.$$

Substituting this value and solving for s,

$$s = \frac{m^2 g}{k^2} (e^{-\frac{k}{m}t} - 1) + \frac{mg}{k} t.$$

24. Motion of the Center of Gravity. — If M is the total mass of a body or system of bodies and F the resultant of all the forces applied to it, the equation

$$F = Ma \qquad\qquad (24)$$

determines the acceleration a of the center of gravity. That is, the center of gravity moves as if the whole mass were concentrated at that point and all the forces applied there.

If all parts of the body move in the same direction with the same velocity, this equation determines the acceleration of any point of the body. If the parts of a complex system, such as a chain, all move along the same path with the same speed, and F is the component of force along the path, (24) gives the acceleration along the path.

25. Motion in a Plane. — When a particle of mass m moves in a plane or in space, its acceleration still satisfies the equation

$$F = ma$$

but the quantities F and a are vectors, that is, have direction as well as magnitude. To obtain an equation whose terms are numbers we project on any line. If the component of F along any line is F_x and the component of a along the same line is a_x, then

$$F_x = ma_x.$$

Suppose the particle moves in a plane. Let (x, y) be its rectangular coördinates. The components of acceleration along the axes are

$$a_x = \frac{d^2x}{dt^2}, \qquad a_y = \frac{d^2y}{dt^2}.$$

If F_x and F_y are the components of force along the axes, the motion of the particle can then be determined by solving the differential equations

$$m \frac{d^2x}{dt^2} = F_x, \qquad m \frac{d^2y}{dt^2} = F_y. \qquad (25a)$$

In problems where the force acts along the line joining the particle to a fixed point it may be more convenient to use polar coördinates with that point as origin. When the particle is at P its acceleration is resolved into a component a_r along OP and a component a_θ perpendicular to OP. These are

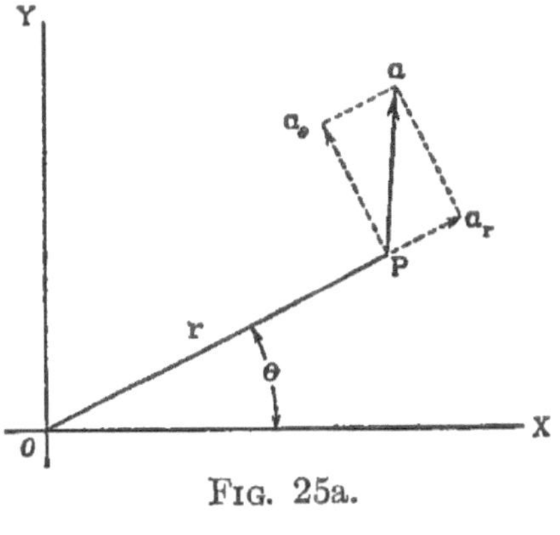

FIG. 25a.

$$a_r = \frac{d^2r}{dt^2} - r\left(\frac{d\theta}{dt}\right)^2 \qquad a_\theta = \frac{1}{r}\frac{d}{dt}\left(r^2\frac{d\theta}{dt}\right). \qquad (25b)$$

If the force acting on the particle has the component F_r along OP and F_θ perpendicular to OP, the motion of the particle can be found by solving the equations

$$ma_r = F_r,$$
$$ma_\theta = F_\theta. \tag{25c}$$

To prove equations (25b) write

$$x = r \cos \theta, \; y = r \sin \theta$$

and calculate

$$a_x = \frac{d^2x}{dt^2}, \qquad a_y = \frac{d^2y}{dt^2}$$

in terms of r and θ. These are accelerations along OX and OY. To obtain a_r project a_x and a_y on OP and add the results. Similarly, to obtain a_θ project on the line perpendicular to OP.

Example 1. When an electron of charge e moves with velocity v in a field of magnetic intensity H, it is pushed sidewise with a force

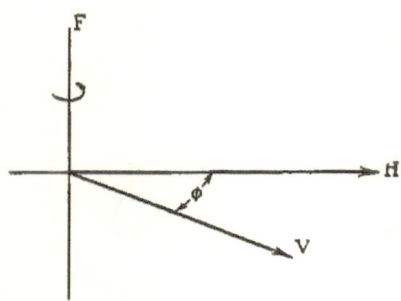

FIG. 25b.

$$F = \frac{e}{c} vH \sin \phi$$

where c is the velocity of light and ϕ the angle between v and H. The force is perpendicular to both v and H and so directed that a right hand rotation about F through the angle ϕ carries v into H.

If H is constant and the electron starts with velocity v_0 in a plane perpendicular to H, find the path described.

Let the electron start at the origin (Fig. 25c) with initial velocity along the x-axis.   Since there is no component of force perpendicular to the xy-plane, it will continue to move in that plane.   Hence $\phi = 90°$ and

$$F = \frac{e}{c} vH.$$

The components of v are

$$\frac{dx}{dt}, \qquad \frac{dy}{dt}.$$

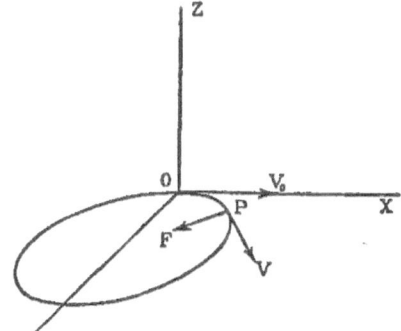

Fig. 25c.

Since F is perpendicular to v and numerically equal to $\frac{e}{c} vH$, its components are

$$-\frac{e}{c} H \frac{dy}{dt}, \qquad \frac{e}{c} H \frac{dx}{dt},$$

the algebraic signs being determined by inspection of the figure.   The equations of motion are therefore

$$m \frac{d^2x}{dt^2} = -\frac{eH}{c} \frac{dy}{dt},$$

$$m \frac{d^2y}{dt^2} = \frac{eH}{c} \frac{dx}{dt}.$$

These equations can be immediately integrated giving

$$m \frac{dx}{dt} = -\frac{eH}{c} y + mv_0,$$

$$m \frac{dy}{dt} = \frac{eH}{c} x,$$

the constants of integration being determined so that

$$x = 0, \quad y = 0, \quad \frac{dx}{dt} = v_0, \quad \frac{dy}{dt} = 0$$

when $t = 0$.   Dividing the second equation by the first

$$\frac{dy}{dx} = \frac{eHx}{cmv_0 - eHy}.$$

Clearing fractions and integrating, we get

$$eH\,(x^2 + y^2) - 2\,cmv_0\,y = 0,$$

the constant being zero since $y = 0$ when $x = 0$.   The electron therefore describes a circle of radius

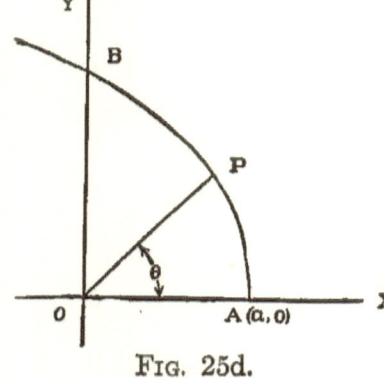

FIG. 25d.

$$\frac{cmv_0}{eH}.$$

Example 2.   A particle of mass m is attracted toward the origin with the force

$$\frac{mk^2}{r^3}.$$

If it starts from the point $(a, 0)$ with velocity $v_0 > \dfrac{k}{a}$ perpendicular to the x-axis, find the motion.

Using polar coördinates, the differential equations are

$$m\left[\frac{d^2r}{dt^2} - r\left(\frac{d\theta}{dt}\right)^2\right] = -\frac{mk^2}{r^3},$$

$$\frac{m}{r}\frac{d}{dt}\left(r^2\frac{d\theta}{dt}\right) = 0.$$

The second equation can be immediately integrated giving

$$r^2\frac{d\theta}{dt} = c_1.$$

At the start $r = a$ and

$$r\frac{d\theta}{dt} = v_0.$$

Hence $c_1 = a v_0$ and

$$\frac{d\theta}{dt} = \frac{a v_0}{r^2}$$

Substituting this value in the first equation

$$\frac{d^2 r}{dt^2} = \frac{a^2 v_0^2 - k^2}{r^3}.$$

multiplying by $\frac{dr}{dt} dt$,

$$\frac{dr}{dt}\frac{d^2 r}{dt^2} dt = \frac{a^2 v_0^2 - k^2}{r^3} dr$$

whence

$$\left(\frac{dr}{dt}\right)^2 = (a^2 v_0^2 - k^2)\left(\frac{1}{a^2} - \frac{1}{r^2}\right),$$

the constant of integration being determined so that $\frac{dr}{dt} = 0$ when $r = a$. Dividing by

$$\left(\frac{d\theta}{dt}\right)^2 = \frac{a^2 v_0^2}{r^4},$$

we obtain

$$\left(\frac{dr}{d\theta}\right)^2 = \frac{a^2 v_0^2 - k^2}{a^4 v_0^2} r^2 (r^2 - a^2).$$

Solving this equation and determining the constant so that $r = a$ when $\theta = 0$, we finally obtain the equation of the curve in the form

$$r = a \sec\left[\frac{\sqrt{a^2 v_0^2 - k^2}}{a v_0}\theta\right].$$

26. Rotation about a Fixed Axis. — Let the body (Fig. 26) rotate about the axis through O perpendicular to the plane AOB. The position of the body can be determined by the angle θ between the fixed line OA and the line OB fixed in the body. The angular velocity of rotation is then

$$\omega = \frac{d\theta}{dt} \qquad (26a)$$

and its angular acceleration

$$\alpha = \frac{d\omega}{dt} = \frac{d^2\theta}{dt^2}. \qquad (26b)$$

Let F be a force in the plane OAB applied to the body at P. The torque about the axis of rotation due to this force is

$$T = Fl,$$

where l is the perpendicular distance from O to the line FP. The torque is positive when the force F tends to increase θ.

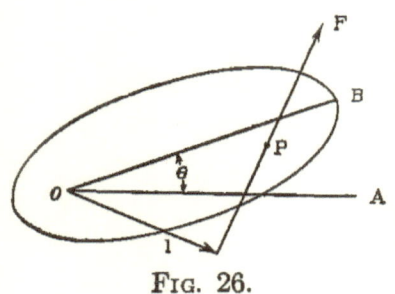

FIG. 26.

The torque and angular acceleration satisfy the equation

$$T = I\alpha, \qquad (26c)$$

where I is the moment of inertia of the body about the axis of rotation and T is the total torque about that axis of all forces acting on the body.

This is analogous to (24), the moment of inertia corresponding to mass and torque corresponding to force.

27. Combined Translation and Rotation. — Consider the motion of a rigid body of mass M whose center of gravity moves in a fixed plane and which at the same time rotates about an axis perpendicular to that plane. In the problems solved here the axis is always an axis of symmetry and the forces acting on the body lie in the fixed plane. The axis of rotation will then remain perpendicular to that plane.

The motion of the center of gravity is determined by the vector equation

$$F = Ma \qquad (27a)$$

and the rotation by the equation

$$T = I\alpha. \qquad (27b)$$

In case of a system consisting of two or more rigid bodies moving as just described there is an equation of the form (27a) and one of the form (27b) for each body. The force F is in each case the resultant of all forces acting on the body. It may not be possible to determine at once the force that two bodies of the system exert on each other. Such a force can be represented by a letter. It will be found that there are enough equations to determine these unknown forces as well as the accelerations.

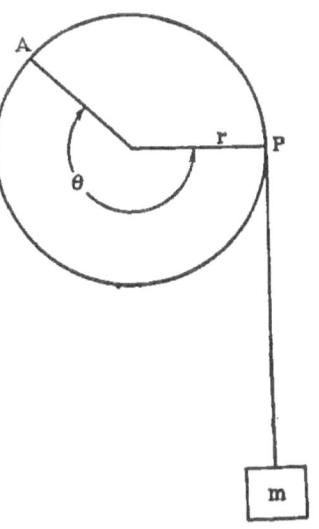

FIG. 27a.

Example 1. A cylinder of mass M and radius r rotates about its axis. A cord wrapped around the cylinder is attached to a mass m which drops vertically. If the cylinder starts from rest, find the angle turned through in t seconds.

Let F be the tension in the cord. The torque about the axis of the cylinder is

$$T = Fr.$$

The moment of inertia of a cylinder is

$$I = \frac{1}{2} Mr^2.$$

Equation (26c) is then

$$\frac{1}{2} Mr^2 \alpha = Fr$$

or

$$\frac{1}{2} Mr \alpha = F. \qquad (1)$$

The forces acting on m are F acting upward and the force of gravity mg acting downward. Its acceleration then satisfies the equation

$$ma = mg - F. \tag{2}$$

If θ is the angle the cylinder turns through in t seconds and s the distance m falls

$$s = r\theta$$

and so

$$\frac{d^2s}{dt^2} = r\frac{d^2\theta}{dt^2},$$

or

$$a = r\alpha \tag{3}$$

By solving (1), (2), (3) simultaneously, we obtain

$$\alpha = \frac{2\,mg}{(M + 2\,m)\,r} = \frac{d^2\theta}{dt^2}.$$

Hence

$$\theta = \frac{mg\,t^2}{(M + 2\,m)\,r}.$$

Example 2. A sphere of mass M and radius r rolls down a plane which makes an angle ϕ with the horizontal. If the coefficient of friction is μ and the inclination is so great that the sphere slides, find its angular acceleration about the horizontal axis through its center of gravity.

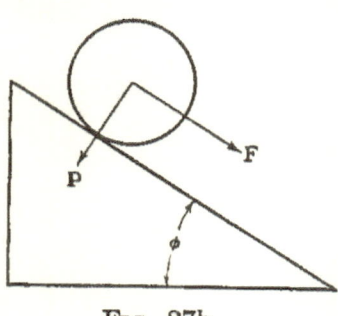

FIG. 27b.

The force of gravity on the sphere can be resolved into two components

$$F = Mg \sin \phi, \qquad P = Mg \cos \phi$$

parallel and perpendicular to the plane. The force of friction is

$$\mu P = \mu\,Mg \cos \phi.$$

The torque due to this force is

$$T = \mu\,Mg\,r \cos \phi.$$

The moment of inertia of a sphere is

$$I = \frac{2}{5} M r^2.$$

Hence

$$\mu \, M \, gr \cos \phi = \frac{2}{5} M r^2 \, \alpha$$

and so

$$\alpha = \frac{5 \, \mu g \, \cos \phi}{2 \, r}.$$

PROBLEMS

1. A beam of length $2\,l$ is supported at its ends and loaded with a weight W at the middle. Find the deflection.

2. Find the deflection of a cantilever beam of length l, held horizontal at one end, and loaded with a weight W at the other end.

3. Find the deflection of a cantilever beam fixed at one end and loaded with a weight w per unit length.

4. Find the deflection of a beam supported at both ends and at the middle point, loaded with a weight w per unit length.

5. Find the deflection of a cantilever beam fixed at one end, supported at the other and loaded with a weight w per unit length.

6. Find the deflection of a beam fixed at both ends and loaded with a weight w per unit length.

7. Consider a vertical column fixed at the base, of length l, and supporting a weight P. Suppose the weight causes the upper end to be displaced the amount a from the vertical. Calculate the bending moment and determine the curve in which the column bends. By substituting the coördinates of the upper end show that the maximum load the column can support is

$$P = \left(\frac{\pi}{2\,l}\right)^2 EI.$$

8. Suppose the ends of the column are rounded but are held in the same vertical line. Find the maximum load the column can support.

9. The cable of a suspension bridge supports a bridge of weight w per unit horizontal distance. Neglecting the weight of the cable find the curve in which it hangs.

10. A series of rods of varying length but the same diameter are hung along a cord. The horizontal distances between consecutive rods are equal and their bottoms are in a straight line. Assuming that they are so close together that the load can be considered continuous, find the curve formed by the cord.

11. A cable is supported by its ends and hangs under its own weight. Find the curve in which it hangs.

12. A telegraph wire weighs 173 lbs. per mile. If the poles are 400 ft. apart and the wire sags 10 ft. at the middle, find the tension at the lowest point of the wire.

13. An arch of a masonry bridge supports a horizontal roadbed and is so constructed that the resultant stress at each point of the arch due to the material above is a compression along the tangent. Find the shape of the arch.

14. A particle of mass m moves in a straight line toward a center of force which attracts with the magnitude

$$\frac{mk^2}{r^3},$$

where r is the distance from the center. If the particle starts from rest at the distance a, find the time required to reach the center.

15. A motor boat weighing 1000 lbs. is moving in a straight line with a velocity of 50 ft./sec. when the motor is shut off. If the resistance of the water is proportional to the velocity of the boat and is equal to 10 lbs. when the velocity is 1 ft./sec., how far will the boat move before the velocity is reduced to 25 ft./sec. How long will be required for this reduction in velocity to take place?

16. A particle of mass m moves toward a fixed center of force which repels with a force k^2m times its distance from the center. If it starts from the distance a with velocity ka, show that it will continually approach but never reach the center.

17. Find the velocity acquired by a body falling from an indefinitely great distance to the earth, assuming that the force of attraction varies inversely as the square of the distance from the center of the earth.

18. Find the time required for a body to fall to the earth from a distance equal to that of the moon. Take the radius of the earth as 4000 mi. and the distance from the center of the earth to the moon as 240,000 miles.

19. If a hole were bored through the center of the earth, a body falling in it would be attracted toward the center with a force proportional to the distance from the center. Find the time required to fall through.

20. A body slides down a rough inclined plane. If the inclination of the plane is α and the coefficient of friction is μ, determine the motion if the particle starts from rest.

21. Assume the resistance of the air proportional to the square of the velocity. If the velocity of a falling body is observed to approach the limiting value 216 ft./sec. and the body starts from rest, find the motion.

22. A particle is projected vertically upward with velocity v_0. Assuming that the resistance of the air is k times the square of the velocity, find the velocity with which it returns to the earth.

23. A chain 6 ft. long starts with 1 ft. of its length hanging over the edge of a smooth table. Neglecting friction, find the time required to slide off.

24. A chain hangs over a smooth peg, 8 ft. of its length being on one side and 10 ft. on the other. Find the time required to slide off.

25. Solve the preceding problem if the force of friction is equal to the weight of 1 ft. of the chain.

26. A projectile is fired with a velocity of 2500 ft./sec. in a direction making 45° with the horizontal. Find the highest point reached and the point where it strikes the ground.

27. A projectile is fired with velocity v_0 at an angle of elevation α. If the resistance of the air is kv, where v is the velocity and k is constant, find the equations of motion.

28. A particle is attracted toward the origin with a force proportional to the distance. If it starts from the point (a, o) with velocity v_0 perpendicular to the x-axis, find the path described.

29. Solve the preceding problem if the particle is repelled with a force proportional to the distance.

30. An electron moves in a magnetic field of intensity H. If it starts with velocity v_0 in a direction making the angle α with H, find the path described (See Example 1, page 44).

31. Prove equations (25b).

32. Determine the orbit of a planet of mass m assuming that it is attracted toward the sun with the force

$$\frac{km}{r^2} ;$$

where r is the distance from the sun. Let r_0 be its distance and v_0 its velocity when nearest the sun.

33. Find the orbit of a comet. Let r_0 be its least distance from the sun and assume that its velocity at an infinite distance is zero.

34. A particle of mass m is attracted toward the origin with the force

$$\frac{k^2 m}{r^5} .$$

If it starts from the point $(a, 0)$ with velocity

$$v_0 = \frac{k}{a^2 \sqrt{2}}$$

perpendicular to the x-axis, find the path described.

35. A circular disk of radius a submerged in oil rotates about the perpendicular axis through its center. Assume the frictional resistance per unit area at each point of the disk to be kv, where v is the velocity of that point and k is constant. If the disk is started with angular velocity ω and the torque due to friction at the bearings is a constant K, find the motion.

36. A ball of radius r rolls without slipping down a plane. If ϕ is the angle of inclination of the plane and the ball starts from rest, find the distance its center moves in t seconds.

37. A billiard ball is started with velocity v_0 not rotating. If the coefficient of friction between the ball and table is μ, find the motion.

38. A cylinder of mass M and radius r rolls on the top of a table. A cord wrapped around the cylinder passes horizontally over a fixed pulley and is attached to a weight m which drops vertically. Find the motion of the cylinder.

39. Solve the preceding problem if the cord is attached to the axis of the cylinder.

40. A wedge shaped block of mass M and 45° angle slides on a smooth table. A mass m slides on its surface. If both start from rest, find the motion.

CHAPTER IV

LINEAR EQUATIONS WITH CONSTANT COEFFICIENTS

28. Equations of the n-th Order. — The solution of an equation of the n-th order in two variables involves n integrations. The general solution therefore contains n constants of integration.

Constants of integration are called *independent* if they occur in the solution in such a way that it is not possible to replace a function of two or more of them by a single constant and so reduce the number of constants. Thus

$$y = c_1 x^2 + c_2 + c_3 \qquad (28)$$

appears to contain 3 constants. We can however take

$$c_2 + c_3 = c$$

and so obtain

$$y = c_1 x^2 + c.$$

It is not possible to further reduce the number. Hence (28) contains two independent constants.

In case of a differential equation of the form

$$\frac{d^n y}{dx^n} = f\left(\frac{d^{n-1} y}{dx^{n-1}}, \cdots, \frac{dy}{dx}, y, x\right),$$

where f is an algebraic function, it can be shown that there is only one solution containing n independent constants of integration. It is called the general solution.

A solution obtained by giving particular values to the constants in the general solution is called a particular solution. Some differential equations have solutions containing less than n constants of integration which are not particular solutions. Such solutions are called singular. They are mainly of mathematical interest and so will not be further considered here.

29. Linear Equations with Constant Coefficients. — A differential equation of the form

$$\frac{d^n y}{dx^n} + a_1 \frac{d^{n-1} y}{dx^{n-1}} + \cdots + a_{n-1} \frac{dy}{dx} + a_n y = f(x) \quad (29a)$$

is called a *linear* equation. By this it is meant that the equation is of first degree in one of the variables (y in this case) and its derivatives. If the coefficients $a_1, a_2, \ldots, a_n$ are constants, it is called a linear equation with constant coefficients. For practical applications this is one of the most important types.

In discussing these equations we shall find it convenient to represent the operation $\frac{d}{dx}$ by D. Then

$$\frac{dy}{dx} = Dy, \qquad \frac{d^2 y}{dx^2} = D^2 y, \text{ etc.}$$

Equation (29a) can be written

$$(D^n + a_1 D^{n-1} + \cdots + a_{n-1} D + a_n) y = f(x). \quad (29b)$$

This signifies that if the operation

$$D^n + a_1 D^{n-1} + \cdots + a_{n-1} D + a_n \quad (29c)$$

is performed on y, the result is $f(x)$. The operation consists in differentiating y, n times, $n - 1$ times, etc., multiplying the results by 1, a_1, a_2, etc., and adding.

With the differential equation is associated an algebraic equation

$$r^n + a_1 r^{n-1} + \cdots + a_{n-1} r + a_n = 0 \quad (29d)$$

having the same coefficients a_1, a_2, etc. as (29a) but with right-hand member zero. If the roots of this *auxiliary* equation are $r_1, r_2, \cdots, r_n$, the polynomial (29c) can be written

$$(D - r_1)(D - r_2) \cdots (D - r_n)$$

and so (29a) has the form

$$(D - r_1) (D - r_2) \cdots (D - r_n) y = f(x). \quad (29e)$$

If we operate on y with $D - r_1$, we get

$$(D - r_1) y = \frac{dy}{dx} - r_1 y.$$

Operating on this with $D - r_2$ we get

$$(D - r_2) (D - r_1) y = (D - r_2) \left(\frac{dy}{dx} - r_1 y \right)$$

$$= \frac{d^2 y}{dx^2} - (r_1 + r_2) y + r_1 r_2 y.$$

The same result is obtained if we operate on y with

$$(D - r_1) (D - r_2) = D^2 - (r_1 + r_2) D + r_1 r_2.$$

Similarly, if we operate in succession with the factors $(D - r_1)$, $(D - r_2)$, etc., in any order whatever we get the same result that we should get by operating directly with the product (29c). It should be noted that this is true only when r_1, r_2, etc., are constant. If the r's are variable it is not in general true that

$$(D - r_1) (D - r_2) y = (D - r_2) (D - r_1) y.$$

30. Equation with Right-hand Member Zero. — To solve the equation

$$(D^n + a_1 D^{n-1} + \cdots + a_{n-1} D + a_n) y = 0, \quad (30a)$$

factor the symbolic operator and so reduce it to the form

$$(D - r_1) (D - r_2) \cdots (D - r_n) y = 0.$$

The value

$$y = c_1 e^{r_1 x}$$

is a solution. For

$$(D - r_1) c_1 e^{r_1 x} = c_1 r_1 e^{r_1 x} - r_1 c_1 e^{r_1 x} = 0,$$

and the equation can be written

$$(D-r_2) \cdots (D-r_n) \cdot (D-r_1) \; y = (D-r_2) \cdots (D-r_n) \cdot 0 = 0.$$

Similarly

$$y = c_2 e^{r_2 x}, \quad y = c_3 e^{r_3 x}, \text{ etc.,}$$

are solutions. Finally

$$y = c_1 e^{r_1 x} + c_2 e^{r_2 x} + \cdots + c_n e^{r_n x} \tag{30b}$$

is a solution; for the result of operating on y is the sum of the results of operating on $c_1 e^{r_1 x}$, $c_2 e^{r_2 x}$, etc., each of which is zero.

If the roots $r_1, r_2, \cdots, r_n$ are all different, (30b) contains n independent constants and so is the general solution of (30a).

If, however, two roots r_1, r_2 are equal

$$c_1 e^{r_1 x} + c_2 e^{r_2 x} = (c_1 + c_2) e^{r_1 x}$$

contains only one constant $c_1 + c_2$ and (30b) contains less than n independent constants. In this case, however, $x e^{r_1 x}$ is a solution; for

$$(D - r_1) \, x e^{r_1 x} = r_1 x e^{r_1 x} + e^{r_1 x} - r_1 x e^{r_1 x} = e^{r_1 x}$$

and so

$$(D - r_1) \, (D - r_2) \, x e^{r_1 x} = (D - r_1)^2 \, x e^{r_1 x} = (D - r_1) \, e^{r_1 x} = 0.$$

If then

$$r_2 = r_1$$

the part of the solution corresponding to these two roots is

$$(c_1 + c_2 x) e^{r_1 x}.$$

More generally, if

$$r_1 = r_2 = \cdots = r_m,$$

the part of the solution corresponding to these m roots is

$$(c_1 + c_2 x + c_3 x^2 + \cdots + c_m x^{m-1}) e^{r_1 x} \tag{30c}$$

If the coefficients $a_1, a_2, \cdots a_n$ are real, imaginary roots occur in pairs

$$r_1 = \alpha + \beta \sqrt{-1}, \qquad r_2 = \alpha - \beta \sqrt{-1}.$$

The terms

$$c_1 e^{r_1 x}, \qquad c_2 e^{r_2 x}$$

are then imaginary but in most problems their sum is real. They can be replaced by two other terms that do not have this imaginary appearance. Using the values of r_1 and r_2 we have

$$(D - r_1)(D - r_2) = (D - \alpha)^2 + \beta^2.$$

By performing the differentiations it can easily be shown that

$$[(D - \alpha)^2 + \beta^2] \cdot e^{\alpha x} \sin \beta x = 0,$$
$$[(D - \alpha)^2 + \beta^2] \cdot e^{\alpha x} \cos \beta x = 0.$$

Therefore

$$e^{\alpha x}[c_1 \cos \beta x + c_2 \sin \beta x] \qquad\qquad (30d)$$

is a solution. This function in which α and β are real can therefore be used as the part of the solution corresponding to two imaginary roots

$$r = \alpha \pm \beta \sqrt{-1}.$$

To solve the differential equation

$$(D^n + a_1 D^{n-1} + \cdots + a_{n-1} D + a_n) y = 0$$

let $r_1, r_2, \cdots, r_n$ be the roots of the auxiliary equation

$$r^n + a_1 r^{n-1} + \cdots + a_{n-1} r + a_n = 0.$$

If these roots are real and different the solution is

$$y = c_1 e^{r_1 x} + c_2 e^{r_2 x} + \cdots + c_n e^{r_n x}.$$

If m of the roots $r_1, r_2, \cdots r_m$ are equal, the corresponding part of the solution is

$$(c_1 + c_2 x + c_3 x^2 + \cdots + c_m x^{m-1}) e^{r_1 x}.$$

The part of the solution corresponding to two imaginary roots $r = \alpha \pm \beta \sqrt{-1}$ *is*

$$e^{\alpha x} [c_1 \cos \beta x + c_2 \sin \beta x].$$

Example 1. $\dfrac{d^2 y}{dx^2} - \dfrac{dy}{dx} - 2y = 0.$

This is equivalent to

$$(D^2 - D - 2) y = 0.$$

The roots of the auxiliary equation

$$r^2 - r - 2 = 0$$

are -1 and 2. Hence the solution is

$$y = c_1 e^{-x} + c_2 e^{2x}$$

Example 2. $\dfrac{d^3 y}{dx^3} + \dfrac{d^2 y}{dx^2} - 5 \dfrac{dy}{dx} + 3y = 0.$

The roots of the auxiliary equation

$$r^3 + r^2 - 5r + 3 = 0$$

are $1, 1, -3$. The part of the solution corresponding to the two roots equal to 1 is

$$(c_1 + c_2 x)e^x.$$

Hence

$$y = (c_1 + c_2 x) e^x + c_3 e^{-3x}.$$

Example 3. $(D^2 + 2D + 2) y = 0.$
The roots of the auxiliary equation are

$$-1 \pm \sqrt{-1}.$$

Therefore

$$\alpha = -1, \ \beta = 1 \text{ in (30d)}$$

and

$$y = e^{-x} [c_1 \cos x + c_2 \sin x].$$

31. Equation with Right-hand Member a Function of x. —
Let $y = u$ be the *general solution* of the equation

$$(D^n + a_1 D^{n-1} + \cdots + a_{n-1} D + a_n) y = 0$$

and let $y = v$ be *any solution* of the equation

$$(D^n + a_1 D^{n-1} + \cdots + a_{n-1}D + a_n) \, y = f(x) \qquad (31)$$

then

$$y = u + v$$

is a solution of (31); for when the operation

$$D^n + a_1 D^{n-1} + \cdots + a_{n-1}D + a_n$$

is performed on u it gives zero and when it is performed on v it gives $f(x)$. Furthermore $u + v$ contains n arbitrary constants. Hence it is the general solution of (31).

The part u is called the *complimentary function*, v the *particular integral*. To solve an equation of the form (31) we first solve the equation with right-hand member zero and then add to the result any solution of (31).

A particular integral can often be found by inspection. If not the general form of the integral can be determined by the following rules:

1. If $f(x) = ax^n + bx^{n-1} + \cdots + p$,

assume

$$y = Ax^n + Bx^{n-1} + \cdots + P,$$

but, if 0 occurs m times as a root of the auxiliary equation, assume

$$y = x^m [Ax^m + Bx^{n-1} + \cdots + P].$$

2. If $f(x) = ce^{ax}$, assume

$$y = Ae^{ax},$$

but, if a occurs m times as a root in the auxiliary equation, assume

$$y = Ax^m e^{ax}.$$

3. If $f(x) = a \cos \beta x + b \sin \beta x$, assume

$$y = A \cos \beta x + B \sin \beta x,$$

but, if $\cos \beta x$ and $\sin \beta x$ occur in the complementary function, assume

$$y = x \left[A \cos \beta x + B \sin \beta x \right].$$

4. If $f(x) = ae^{\alpha x} \cos \beta x + be^{\alpha x} \sin \beta x$, assume

$$y = Ae^{\alpha x} \cos \beta x + Be^{\alpha x} \sin \beta x,$$

but, if $e^{\alpha x} \cos \beta x$ and $e^{\alpha x} \sin \beta x$ occur in the complementary function, assume

$$y = xe^{\alpha x} \left[A \cos \beta x + B \sin \beta x \right].$$

If $f(x)$ contains terms of different types, take for y the sum of the corresponding expressions. Substitute the assumed value of y in the differential equation and determine the constants A, B, C, etc., so that the equation is satisfied.

The general principle in the above rules is to express y as a linear function of all the distinct kinds of functions in $f(x)$ and its derivatives of all orders. The exceptions to the various rules occur when some of the terms in the assumed value of y occur in the complementary function.

Example 1. $\dfrac{d^2y}{dx^2} + 4y = 2x + 3.$

A particular integral is evidently

$$y = \frac{1}{4}(2x + 3).$$

The solution of

$$\frac{d^2y}{dx^2} + 4y = 0$$

is

$$y = c_1 \cos 2x + c_2 \sin 2x.$$

Hence the solution of the original equation is

$$y = c_1 \cos 2x + c_2 \sin 2x + \frac{1}{4}(2x + 3).$$

Example 2. $(D^2 + 3D + 2)y = 2 + e^{-x}$

Assume
$$y = A + Be^x.$$

Substituting this value for y
$$2A + 6Be^x = 2 + e^x.$$

Hence
$$2A = 2, \quad 6B = 1$$

and
$$A + Be^x = 1 + \frac{1}{6}e^x.$$

Hence
$$y = 1 + \frac{1}{6}e^x + c_1 e^{-x} + c_2 e^{-2x}.$$

Example 3. $\dfrac{d^3y}{dx^3} + \dfrac{d^2y}{dx^2} = x^2.$

The roots of the auxiliary equation are $0, 0, -1$.
Since 0 is twice a root, we assume
$$y = x^2 (Ax^2 + Bx + c).$$

Substituting this value,
$$12Ax^2 + (24A + 6B)x + 6B + 2c = x^2.$$

Consequently
$$12A = 1, \quad 24A + 6B = 0, \quad 6B + 2c = 0,$$

whence
$$A = \frac{1}{12}, \quad B = -\frac{1}{3}, \quad c = 1.$$

The solution is
$$y = \frac{1}{12}x^4 - \frac{1}{3}x^3 + x^2 + c_1 + c_2 x + c_3 e^{-x}.$$

32. Simultaneous Linear Equations. — We consider only linear equations with constant coefficients, containing one independent variable and as many dependent variables as equations. All but one of the dependent variables can be eliminated by a process analogous to that used in solving linear algebraic equations. The one remaining dependent variable is the solution of a linear equation. Its value can be found and the other dependent variables can then be determined by substituting in the preceding equations.

If possible the work should be so arranged that after the first variable is found the others can be determined without integration. If integration is used in determining these later variables, the constants of integration may not all be arbitrary. It is then necessary to substitute the values found in the differential equations to determine the relations between the constants.

Example. $\dfrac{d^2x}{dt^2} - 3x - y = e^t$

$\dfrac{dy}{dt} - 2x = 0.$

Using D for $\dfrac{d}{dt}$, these equations can be written

$$(D^2 - 3)x - y = e^t$$
$$-2x + Dy = 0$$

Multiplying the first equation by 2 and the second by $D^2 - 3$, we have

$$2(D^2 - 3)x - 2y = 2e^t,$$
$$-2(D^2 - 3)x + (D^2 - 3)Dy = 0.$$

Adding, we get

$$(D^3 - 3D - 2)y = 2e^t.$$

This equation, containing only one dependent variable, can be solved for y giving

$$y = (c_1 + c_2 t)e^{-t} + c_3 e^{2t} - \frac{1}{2}e^t.$$

Substituting this value of y in the second equation, we find

$$x = \frac{1}{2}Dy = \frac{1}{2}\left[(c_2 - c_1) - c_2 t\right]e^{-t} + c_3 e^{2t} - \frac{1}{4}e^t.$$

EXERCISES

1. $\dfrac{d^2y}{dx^2} - \dfrac{dy}{dx} = 0.$

2. $\dfrac{d^2y}{dx^2} + 2\dfrac{dy}{dx} - 3y = 0.$

3. $\dfrac{d^2y}{dx^2} - 4\dfrac{dy}{dx} + 4y = 0.$

4. $\dfrac{d^2y}{dx^2} + y = 0.$

5. $\dfrac{d^3y}{dx^3} - 2\dfrac{d^2y}{dx^2} - 3\dfrac{dy}{dx} = 0.$

6. $\dfrac{d^4y}{dx^4} = y.$

7. $\dfrac{d^2y}{dx^2} - 2\dfrac{dy}{dx} + 2y = 0.$

8. $\dfrac{d^2y}{dx^2} + \dfrac{dy}{dx} + y = 0.$

9. $\dfrac{d^3y}{dx^3} + 3\dfrac{d^2y}{dx^2} + 3\dfrac{dy}{dx} + y = 0.$

10. $\dfrac{d^2y}{dx^2} + y = 2 - x.$

11. $\dfrac{d^2y}{dx^2} - 4y = x^2.$

12. $\dfrac{dy}{dx} - y = \sin x.$

13. $\dfrac{d^2y}{dx^2} - \dfrac{dy}{dx} = x.$

14. $\dfrac{d^2y}{dx^2} + 4\dfrac{dy}{dx} + 3y = x + e^{2x}.$

15. $\dfrac{d^2y}{dx^2} - a^2y = e^{ax}.$

16. $\dfrac{d^2y}{dx^2} + a^2y = \cos ax.$

17. $\dfrac{d^3y}{dx^3} - y = x^3 - 1.$

18. $\dfrac{d^2y}{dx^2} - 4\dfrac{dy}{dx} + 3y = e^{2x}\sin x.$

19. $\dfrac{d^2y}{dx^2} - 9y = e^{3x}\cos x.$

20. $\dfrac{d^4y}{dx^4} + \dfrac{d^3y}{dx^3} = \cos 4x.$

21. $\dfrac{d^2y}{dx^2} + 2\dfrac{dy}{dx} + y = e^x + e^{-x}.$

22. $\dfrac{dx}{dt} = y + 1, \quad \dfrac{dy}{dt} = x + 1.$

23. $\dfrac{dx}{dt} = x - 2y, \dfrac{dy}{dt} = x - y.$

24. $4\dfrac{dx}{dt} - \dfrac{dy}{dt} + 3x = \sin t, \quad \dfrac{dx}{dt} + y = \cos t.$

25. $\dfrac{d^2y}{dt^2} = x, \quad \dfrac{d^2x}{dt^2} = y.$

26. $\dfrac{d^2x}{dt^2} + \dfrac{dy}{dt} + x = e^t, \quad \dfrac{dx}{dt} + \dfrac{d^2y}{dt^2} = 1.$

33. Vibrating Systems. — When a body is given a slight displacement from a position of stable equilibrium and released, it vibrates about the position of equilibrium.

If the resistance is neglected the differential equation of motion usually has the form

$$\frac{d^2x}{dt^2} + k^2x = 0.$$

The solution of this equation can be written

$$x = A \cos (kt + \theta), \tag{33a}$$

when A and θ are constants. The motion is called *harmonic*. A is called the *amplitude* and θ the *phase* angle. In a complete vibration (across and back) the angle

$$kt + \theta$$

increases 360°, or 2π. The time of vibration is therefore

$$T = \frac{2\pi}{k}.$$

If the resistance is proportional to the velocity, the differential equation has the form

$$\frac{d^2x}{dt^2} + a\frac{dx}{dt} + b = 0.$$

The solution of this equation has the form

$$x = Ae^{-\alpha t} \cos (\beta t + \theta). \tag{33b}$$

If at time t, the body is at the end of a swing,

$$Ae^{-\alpha t}$$

is the amplitude of that swing. The amplitude thus decreases with the time.

In some cases the differential equation has the form

$$\frac{d^2\theta}{dt^2} + k^2 \sin \theta = 0.$$

This is not a linear equation. It becomes linear, however, if we replace $\sin \theta$ by θ. For small angles this is a good approximation. Thus, when the angle is 5°

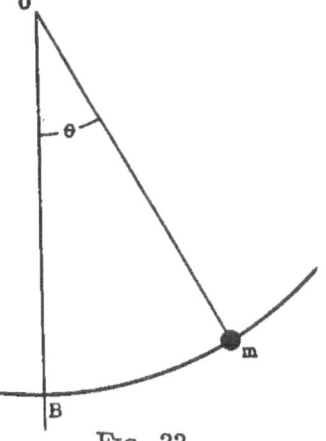

$$\sin \theta = .08716,$$
$$\theta = .08727,$$

showing that the error is less than 1 part in 800. Even for angles of 10° the error is only about $\frac{1}{2}$ per cent.

Example. A pendulum, consisting of a particle of mass m supported by a string of length l, swings in a medium which resists

Fig. 33.

with a force proportional to the velocity. Find the time of vibration.

The torque about the point of suspension due to the weight of m is

$$- mg \sin \theta$$

the negative sign being used because when θ is positive the torque tends to decrease θ. The velocity of m is

$$v = l\frac{d\theta}{dt}.$$

The resistance is then

$$kl\frac{d\theta}{dt}.$$

The torque due to this resistance is

$$- kl \cdot \frac{d\theta}{dt} \cdot l,$$

the negative sign being used since when $\frac{d\theta}{dt}$ is positive the torque is negative.   The moment of inertia of m about 0 is ml^2.

The equation

$$I \frac{d^2\theta}{dt^2} = T$$

is therefore

$$ml^2 \frac{d^2\theta}{dt} = - mg\, l \sin \theta - kl^2 \frac{d\theta}{dt}.$$

Replacing $\sin \theta$ by θ, this becomes

$$\frac{d^2\theta}{dt^2} + \frac{k}{m}\frac{d\theta}{dt} + \frac{g}{l}\theta = 0.$$

The solution of this equation has the form

$$\theta = A e^{-\frac{kt}{2m}} \cos\left[t\sqrt{\frac{g}{l} - \frac{k^2}{4\,m^2}} + \alpha\right].$$

The period of vibration is therefore

$$T = \frac{2\pi}{\sqrt{\dfrac{g}{l} - \dfrac{k^2}{4\,m^2}}}.$$

PROBLEMS

1. Reduce the expression

$$x = c_1 \cos kt + c_2 \sin kt$$

to the form

$$x = A \cos (kt + \theta).$$

Find A and θ in terms of c_1 and c_2.

2. Reduce the expression

$$x = e^{-\alpha t} [c_1 \cos \beta t + c_2 \sin \beta t]$$

to the form (33b).

3. The force exerted by a spring is proportional to the amount the spring is stretched and is 2 lbs. when the spring is stretched $\frac{1}{2}$ in. A mass of 5 lbs. is suspended by the spring. If the mass is depressed slightly and released, find the time of vibration.

4. A disk of radius a and mass M is supported in a horizontal plane by a vertical wire attached to its center. When the disk is rotated about the vertical axis through the angle θ the torque exerted by the wire is

$$T = k\theta$$

When the disk is rotated through a small angle and released it vibrates n times per second. Find the constant k.

5. A cylindrical spar buoy stands vertically in the water. Its diameter is 12 in. and its mass 200 lbs. Find the time of vibration when it is depressed slightly and released.

6. Two equal weights are hanging at the end of an elastic string. One falls off. Find the motion of the remaining weight.

7. One end of an elastic string of natural length a is attached to a fixed point on a horizontal table and to the other end a mass m is attached. If m is drawn aside until the string is elongated the amount a and released, find the time of one complete vibration if a force of P lbs. elongates the string 1 ft.

8. A 10-lb. body is observed to vibrate 90 times per minute and the oscillation damps to $\frac{1}{2}$ amplitude in 15 secs. Find the differential equation of motion.

9. A 10-lb. mass is acted upon by a restitutive force proportional to the displacement and equal to 2 lbs. when the displacement is 1 ft. Find the period if the vibration damps to $\frac{1}{10}$ amplitude after 3 complete vibrations.

10. A rod of length $2\,l$ is supported in a horizontal position by two vertical strings of length l attached to its ends. If the rod is turned through a small angle about the vertical line through its center and released, find the time of vibration.

11. A rod of length $2\,l$ rests in a horizontal position on a cylinder of radius a. If it is tipped slightly, find the time of vibration.

12. If C is the capacity of a condenser the electromotive force across the condenser is

$$\frac{1}{C}\int i\, dt.$$

If a constant electromotive force E is impressed on a circuit containing a resistance R, inductance L, and capacity C, find the current as a function of the time if $i = 0$ and $\int i\, dt = 0$ when $t = 0$. (See Prob. 3, page 31.)

13. A wire of length l and mass m is fastened by one end and rotated with angular velocity ω in a horizontal plane. If under a force F it stretches the amount klF, find the amount it is stretched by centrifugal force.

14. A horizontal tube rotates about a vertical axis with angular velocity ω. A ball inside the tube and sliding without friction starts from the center with velocity v_0. Find its motion.

15. A particle of mass m is attracted toward each of two centers of force with a force equal to k times the distance. If the distance between the two centers is $2b$ and the particle starts from rest at the point on the joining line at distance c from the center, find its motion.

16. In the preceding problem find the motion if the particle starts with velocity v_0 perpendicular to the line joining the centers of force.

17. When a current i flows through a resistance R the drop in potential is iR. When a potential E is impressed on a region of leakance G, the current that leaks away is EG. If the resistance of a cable is r per unit length and its leakance g per unit length, what current and potential must a line of length l receive at one end if the current and potential at the other end are to be I_0 and E_0.

18. A helical spring of natural length $2l$ and negligible mass is hung up by one end. Two equal weights of mass m are attached, one at the middle, the other at the lower end, and let fall. Find the motion if when hanging at rest the weights stretch the spring the amount c.

19. A weight of 4 lbs. is suspended by a spring. The weight extends the spring 1 inch. If the upper end of the spring is given the harmonic motion

$$y = \sin(\sqrt{\overline{12g\,t}})$$

in the vertical line, find the motion of the suspended weight.

20. Two weights of 4 lbs. are connected by the spring of the preceding problem, one of the weights being held fixed and the other suspended by the spring. If the upper weight is released, find the motion of the two weights.

21. According to Newton's law the gravitational attraction between two masses m_1, m_2 at distance d is

$$k\,\frac{m_1 m_2}{d^2}.$$

Find the motion of the two masses assuming that their center of gravity remains fixed.

ANSWERS

Pages **3, 4**

1. $\tan^2 x - \cot^2 y = c.$
2. $1 + y^2 = c(1 - x^2).$
3. $x^2 y^2 + x^2 - y^2 = c.$
4. $y + a = c \sin x.$

5. $x = \ln \dfrac{c}{e^y - 1}.$

6. $x = c \dfrac{y - 1}{y}.$

Pages **14–18**

1. $y^2 = cx.$
2. $y = \sqrt{4 - x^2} + 2\ln\left(\dfrac{2 - \sqrt{4 - x^2}}{x}\right).$
3. $y = 5.66\, y_0$ 4. $R = R_0\, e^{-.1733t}$
5. $\omega = 100\, e^{-1.12t}$ revolutions per minute.
6. 1 hr.
7. $x_0 = 56.5.$ 7.84 hrs.
9. Parabola.
10. Paraboloid of revolution.
11. Hyperboloid of revolution.
12. 10 years.
13. About $11\frac{1}{2}$ years.
14. $\frac{1}{2}klW.$
15. $(P + \frac{1}{2}W)\, kl.$
16. $p = 14.7\, e^{-.00004h}$
17. About $17\frac{1}{2}$ miles.
19. $T_2 - \dfrac{wv^2}{g} = \left(T_1 - \dfrac{wv^2}{g}\right)e^{\mu\alpha}.$

22. 9.8 min.
23. 10.2 min.
24. 4 min.
25. 18.4.
26. 4.6 min.
27. 6.6 days.
28. 19.5 lbs.
29. 54.7 lbs.
30. 99.5 %.
31. 1500 cu. ft.
32. .24%.
33. .124%.
34. $T = \frac{2}{3}x.$ 864,000 cal.

35. $T = 592 - 187.6\ln r.$ 1,731,000 cal.
36. .0005
37. $\dfrac{1}{1024}.$
38. 2.8 lbs

39. 2.9 days.
40. 15.5 lbs.
41. 50 min.

Pages **29, 30**

1. $x^3 + x^2 y - xy^2 - y^3 = c.$
2. $x^3 = 3xy + c.$
3. $x^3 + 3xy^2 = c.$
4. $x^2 - y^2 = cx.$

5. $2xy + y^2 = c.$
6. $\dfrac{x}{y} - \ln y = c.$
7. $y(1 + cx) = 1$

8. $y = \dfrac{e^{bx}}{b - a} + ce^{ax}$.

9. $y = \dfrac{1}{x}(cx^3 - 1)$.

10. $y = cx^2e^{-3/x}$.

11. $y = \dfrac{x}{x^2 - c}$.

12. $y + a = c \sin x$.

13. $x^4 + 4y(x^2 - 1)^{\frac{3}{2}} = c$

14. $x = y^2(c - e^{-y})$.

15. $e^{\frac{x}{y}} + \ln x = c$.

16. $\dfrac{1}{y^2} = x + \frac{1}{2} + ce^{2x}$.

17. $x^3 = y(\frac{1}{7}x^7 + c)$.

18. $\ln(x^2 + y^2) = 2\tan^{-1}\dfrac{y}{x} + c$.

19. $y^2 - 1 = c(1 + x)^2e^{-2x}$.

20. $y = \dfrac{c}{2}x^2 - \dfrac{1}{2c}$

21. $y \sin x + \frac{1}{2}y^2 - \frac{1}{3}x^3 = c$.

22. $y = \frac{1}{2}x[e^{x+c} - e^{-x-c}]$.

23. $(2y - x)\sqrt{1 + x^2} = c - \ln(x + \sqrt{x^2 + 1})$.

24. $y^4 = 4xy + c$.

25. $y^2 = \frac{2}{3}\sin x + c\csc^2 x$.

26. $x + 2y + \ln(x + y - 2) = c$.

27. $y^3 = ce^x - x - 1$.

28. $y = \dfrac{c}{2}x^2 - \dfrac{1}{2c}$.

29. $y = ce^x$ or $y = c + \frac{1}{2}x^2$.

30. $e^{2x} - 2e^{x+y} = c$.

31. $x + 2y + 3\ln(2x + 3y - 7) = c$.

32. $(x + y)^2 = cx^3e^{-\frac{x}{x+y}}$.

33. $x = \frac{1}{2}e^t + c_1e^{-t}$, $y = \frac{1}{2}e^t - c_1e^{-t} + c_2$.

34. $x = c_1e^{-t} + c_2e^t + 1$, $y = c_1e^{-t} - c_2e^t + 1$.

35. $y = c_1e^{\frac{1}{2}t} + c_2e^{\frac{1}{3}t}$, $x = 4c_1e^{\frac{1}{2}t} + 3c_2e^{\frac{1}{3}t}$.

36. $x = c_1e^{-t} + c_2e^{-3t}$, $y = c_1e^{-t} + 3c_2e^{-3t} + \cos t$.

Pages 31, 32

2. 14.9 lbs.

3. $i = \dfrac{E}{R^2 + L^2\omega^2}\left[R \sin \omega t - L\omega \cos \omega t + L\omega e^{-\frac{R}{L}t}\right]$.

4. $i_1 = \dfrac{I}{R^2 + L^2\omega^2}\Big[(RR_2 + LL_2\omega^2)\sin \omega t$

$$+ \omega(L_2R - R_2L)(\cos \omega t - e^{-\frac{R}{L}t})\Big],$$

where $R = R_1 + R_2$, $L = L_1 + L_2$.

5. $rp = c(e^{\frac{1}{2}k\omega^2 r^2} - 1)$, c, k being constants.

6. $x = \frac{1}{4}(1 - 2^{-t})$, $y = \frac{3}{4}(1 - 2^{-t})$.

7. $y = 4.5(1 - e^{-.7324t})$, $x = 10 - y$.

8. $B = .214$, $c = .249$.

9. $\left(1 + \dfrac{a}{r}\right)\sin \theta = c$.

Page 36

1. $y = x \ln x + \frac{1}{6}x^3 + c_1x + c_2$.

2. $y = c_1 \ln x + c_2 - \frac{1}{4}x^2$.

3. $y = \frac{1}{6}(x + a)^3 + c_1x + c_2$.

4. $y = c_1e^x + c_2e^{-x}$.

5. $y = c_1 \cos(kx + c_2)$.

6. $c_1 t + c_2 = \sqrt{s\,(c_1 s + 2\,k^2)} + \dfrac{k^2}{\sqrt{-c_1}}\,\sin^{-1}\left(\dfrac{c_1 s + k^2}{k^2}\right)$ if $c_1 < 0$.

7. $e^{a2s} = \dfrac{c_1}{2}\,[e^{abt+c_2} + e^{-abt-c_2}]$.

8. $y = \frac{1}{4}\,c_1 x^2 - \dfrac{1}{2\,c_1}\ln x + c_2$.

9. $y = x + c_1 x e^x + c_2$.

11. $y = \frac{1}{2}\,(\ln x)^2 + c_1 \ln x + c_2$.

10. $y = \frac{1}{2}\,(e^{c_1 x + c_2} + e^{-c_1 x - c_2})$.

12. $c_1 s^2 = a^2 + (c_1 t + c_2)^2$.

Pages 51–54

1. $EIy = \frac{1}{4}\,W\,(lx^2 - \frac{1}{3}\,x^3)$, the origin being the middle point

2. $EIy = \frac{1}{2}\,W\,(\frac{1}{3}\,x^3 - lx^2)$, the fixed end being the origin.

3. $EIy = -\dfrac{1}{24}\,w\,(6\,l^2 x^2 - 4\,lx^3 + x^4)$.

4. $EIy = \dfrac{1}{24}\,w\,[3\,l^2 x^2 - 2\,lx^3 - x^4]$, the length being $2\,l$.

5. The same as Prob. 4 if the length is l.

6. $EIy = \dfrac{w}{24}\,[2\,l^2 x^2 - x^4]$.

8. $P = \left(\dfrac{\pi}{l}\right)^2 EI$.

9. Parabola.

10. $y = c\,(e^{kx} + e^{-kx})$

11. $y = \dfrac{a}{2}\left(e^{\frac{x}{a}} + e^{-\frac{x}{a}}\right)$, if the axes are properly chosen.

12. 65.5 lbs.

13. Parabola.

14. $\dfrac{a^2}{k}$.

15. 77.6 ft.   2.15 sec.

17. About 7 miles per second.

18. 116 hours.

19. About $42\frac{1}{2}$ min.

20. $s = \frac{1}{2}\,g\,(\sin \alpha - \mu \cos \alpha)\,t^2$.

21. $s = \dfrac{(216)^2}{g}\left[\dfrac{e^{\frac{gt}{2\,6}} + e^{-\frac{gt}{2\,6}}}{2}\right]$.

22. $v_0 \sqrt{\dfrac{mg}{mg + kv_0^2}}$.

23. $t = \sqrt{\dfrac{6}{g}}\ln\,(6 + \sqrt{35})$.

24. $t = \dfrac{3}{\sqrt{g}}\ln\,(9 + 4\,\sqrt{5})$.

25. $t = \dfrac{3}{\sqrt{g}}\cdot\ln\,(17 + 4\,\sqrt{18})$.

26. Maximum height 48,500 ft., range 36.7 mi.

27. $x = \dfrac{mv_0 \cos \alpha}{k}\,(1 - e^{-\frac{k}{m}t})$,

$y = \dfrac{m}{k^2}\,(kv_0 \sin \alpha + mg)\,(1 - e^{-\frac{k}{m}}) - \dfrac{mgt}{k}$.

28. $\dfrac{x^2}{a^2} + \dfrac{ky^2}{mv_0^2} = 1$.

29. $\dfrac{x^2}{a^2} - \dfrac{ky^2}{mv_0^2} = 1$.

30. Helix.

32.   The ellipse, $\dfrac{\bar{1}}{r} = \left(\dfrac{1}{r_0} - \dfrac{k}{r_0^2 v_0^2} \right) \cos \theta + \dfrac{k}{r_0^2 v_0^2}$.

33. $r = \dfrac{2\,r_0}{1 + \cos \theta}$.   34. $r = a \cos \theta$.

35. $\theta = \dfrac{m}{\pi\,ka^2} \left(\omega + \dfrac{2\,K}{\pi\,ka^4} \right) \left(1 - e^{-\frac{\pi ka^2 t}{m}} \right) - \dfrac{2\,Kt}{\pi\,ka^4}$.

36. $\dfrac{5}{14}\, gt^2 \sin \phi$.

37.   It slides until $t = \dfrac{2\,v_0}{7\mu g}$ and then rolls.

38. $a = \dfrac{4\,mg}{8\,m + 3\,M}$.   39. $a = \dfrac{2\,mg}{2\,m + 3\,M}$.

40.   The distance M moves in t seconds is $\dfrac{mgt^2}{2\,m + 4\,M}$.

Pages 65, 66

1. $y = c_1 + c_2 e^x$.   4. $y = c_1 \cos x + c_2 \sin x$.

2. $y = c_1 e^x + c_2 e^{3x}$.   5. $y = c_1 + c_2 e^{-x} + c_3 e^{3x}$.

3. $y = (c_1 + c_2 x)e^{2x}$.

6. $y = c_1 e^x + c_2 e^{-x} + c_3 \sin x + c_4 \cos x$.

7. $y = e^x\,[c_1 \cos x + c_2 \sin x]$.

8. $y = e^{-\frac{1}{2}x}\,[c_1 \cos (\tfrac{1}{2}\sqrt{3}\,x) + c_2 \sin (\tfrac{1}{2}\sqrt{3}\,x).]$

9. $y = (c_1 + c_2 x + c_3 x^2)e^{-x}$.

10. $y = 2 - x + c_1 \cos x + c_2 \sin x$.

11. $y = c_1 e^{2x} + c_2 e^{-2x} - \tfrac{1}{4} x^2 - \tfrac{1}{8}$.

12. $y = c_1 e^x - \tfrac{1}{2}\,(\sin x + \cos x)$.

13. $y = c_1 + c_2 e^x - \tfrac{1}{2} x^2 - x$.

14. $y = c_1 e^{-x} + c_2 e^{-3x} + \tfrac{1}{3} x - \dfrac{4}{9} + \dfrac{1}{15}\, e^{2x}$.

15. $y = c_1 e^{ax} + c_2 e^{-ax} + \dfrac{1}{2\,a}\, x e^{ax}$.

16. $y = \left(c_1 + \dfrac{x}{2\,a} \right) \sin ax + c_2 \cos ax$.

17. $y = c_1 e^x + e^{-\frac{1}{2}x} \left(c_2 \cos \dfrac{x\,\sqrt{3}}{2} + c_3 \sin \dfrac{x\,\sqrt{3}}{2} \right) - x^3 - 5$

18. $y = c_1 e^x + c_2 e^{3x} - \tfrac{1}{2}\, e^{2x} \sin x$.

19. $y = c_1 e^{3x} + c_2 e^{-3x} + \dfrac{1}{37} e^{3x} (6 \sin x - \cos x)$.

20. $y = c_1 + c_2 x + c_3 x^2 + c_4 e^{-x} + \dfrac{1}{1088} (4 \cos 4\,x - \sin 4\,x)$.

21. $y = (c_1 + c_2 x + \tfrac{1}{2} x^2) e^{-x} + \tfrac{1}{4} e^x$.

22. $y = c_1 e^t + c_2 e^{-t} - 1$, $\quad x = c_1 e^t - c_2 e^{-t} - 1$.

23. $y = c_1 \cos t + c_2 \sin t$, $\quad x = (c_1 + c_2) \cos t + (c_2 - c_1) \sin t$.

24. $x = c_1 e^{-t} + c_2 e^{-3t}$, $\quad y = c_1 e^{-t} + 3 c_2 e^{-3t} + \cos t$.

25. $x = c_1 e^t + c_2 e^{-t} + c_3 \cos t + c_4 \sin t$,

    $y = c_1 e^t + c_2 e^{-t} - c_3 \cos t - c_4 \sin t$.

26. $x = c_1 + c_2 t + c_3 t^2 - \tfrac{1}{6} t^3 + e^t$

    $y = c_4 - (c_1 + 2 c_3) t - \tfrac{1}{2} (c_2 - 1) t^2 - \tfrac{1}{3} c_3 t^3 + \dfrac{1}{24} t^4 - e^t$.

Pages 68–70

3. $\dfrac{\pi}{2} \sqrt{\dfrac{5}{3\,g}}$.

4. $k = 2\,\pi^2 n^2 M a^2$.

5. 2.24 sec.

6. $x = a \cos \left(\sqrt{\dfrac{g}{a}} t \right)$, where a is the amount the string is stretched by one weight and x is measured from the point where it would hang in equilibrium.

7. $(4 + 2\,\pi) \sqrt{\dfrac{m}{p}}$.

8. $\dfrac{d^2x}{dt^2} + .0924 \dfrac{dx}{dt} + 88.83\, x = 0$.

9. 2.49 sec.

10. $2\,\pi \sqrt{\dfrac{l}{3\,g}}$.

11. $\dfrac{2\,\pi l}{\sqrt{3\,ag}}$.

12. $i = \dfrac{2\,CE}{\sqrt{4\,LE - C^2 R^2}} e^{-\frac{Rl}{2L}} \sin t \dfrac{\sqrt{4\,LC - C^2 R^2}}{2\,LC}$.

13. $l \left(\dfrac{\tan \theta}{\theta} - 1 \right)$, where $\theta = \omega \sqrt{kml}$.

14. $r = \dfrac{v_0}{2\,\omega} (e^{\omega t} - e^{-\omega t})$.

15. $x = c \cos t \sqrt{\dfrac{2k}{m}}$, the origin being midway between the centers.

16. An ellipse.

17. $i = \frac{1}{2}\left(I_0 + E_0 \sqrt{\dfrac{g}{r}}\right)e^{t\sqrt{rg}} + \frac{1}{2}\left(I_0 - E_0 \sqrt{\dfrac{g}{r}}\right)e^{-t\sqrt{rg}}.$

INDEX

The numbers refer to the pages

www.ingramcontent.com/pod-product-compliance
Lightning Source LLC
Chambersburg PA
CBHW021231280526
45784CB00005B/2056